THE MACMILLAN SHAKESPEARE
GENERAL EDITOR: PETER HOLLINDALE,
Senior Lecturer in English and Education,
University of York
ADVISORY EDITOR: PHILIP BROCKBANK,
Professor of English, University of York

JULIUS CAESAR

Other titles in the series

THE MACMILLAN SHAKESPEARE

JULIUS CAESAR

Edited by
D. R. Elloway

MACMILLAN EDUCATION

First published 1974
Reprinted 1975, 1977, 1978, 1979

Published by
MACMILLAN EDUCATION LTD
Houndmills Basingstoke Hampshire RG21 2XS
and London
Associated companies in Delhi Dublin
Hong Kong Johannesburg Lagos Melbourne
New York Singapore and Tokyo

Printed in Hong Kong

CONTENTS

PREFACE

All editions of *Julius Caesar* must be based on the text as it was first published in the 1623 collected edition of Shakespeare's plays, known as the First Folio. Some of the more probable emendations suggested by later editors have been accepted for this edition, and the more important of these are referred to in the notes. The spelling and punctuation have been modernised, but something of the weight of the original punctuation has been retained.

The editor is deeply indebted to the many previous editors and interpreters of the play, in particular to T. S. Dorsch for his edition of *Julius Caesar* in the Arden Shakespeare.

D.R.E.

INTRODUCTION

POLITICAL ISSUES

In 1599 Thomas Platter, a Swiss traveller visiting London, wrote in his journal:

> After lunch on September 21st, at about two o'clock, I and my party crossed the river, and there in the house with the thatched roof we saw an excellent performance of the tragedy of the first Emperor Julius Caeser with about fifteen characters; after the play, according to their custom they did a most elegant and curious dance, two dressed in men's clothes, and two in women's.

The 'house with the thatched roof' was almost certainly the newly-built Globe theatre, and the play, Shakespeare's *Julius Caesar*, which may have been written for the opening of the Globe. It rapidly became one of the most popular of his plays.

Julius Caesar was the first of the sequence of tragedies that Shakespeare was to write in the first decade of the seventeenth century, ending with *Antony and Cleopatra*, which follows the later fortunes of Antony and his rivalry with Octavius that is hinted at in the earlier play (V. i. 16–20). It differs in a number of ways from the tragedies that follow it. It has no distinct hero or villain, and the climax comes in Act Three. If Brutus were the hero, the climax would be his death – as is the death of Macbeth after he, too, has carried out a political assassination earlier in the play – but in *Julius Ceasar* the overwhelming impression is that the last two acts are working out the consequences of the murder of Caesar and of the reversal of fortunes produced by Antony's speech to the crowd. It is very much a political play, like the history plays that immediately preceded it. It is concerned with public events and with its characters as public figures; we know them also as private individuals, and the play continually relates their personal characters and lives to their public offices and responsibilities,

2

but it does not penetrate deeply into their inner natures as does *Macbeth* or *Hamlet* or *King Lear*.

Julius Caesar also deals with the same themes as the histories – the nature of authority in the state and the dangers of tyranny, usurpation and civil war. These were matters of urgent concern at the end of the sixteenth century, as Elizabeth's long reign drew to its close with no direct heir to succeed her – which may be reflected in Caesar's desire for an heir (I. ii. 1–9). There was the danger that the accession of James I would be disputed and that powerful nobles might try to seize the throne. The chief threat in 1599 came from Robert Devereux, Earl of Essex, the unstable, ambitious and immensely popular favourite of the Queen. Earlier in the year he had gone to Ireland with a large army to put down Tyrone's rebellion, and the enthusiastic farewell given him by the London mob may have inspired Shakespeare's description of the Roman crowd welcoming Pompey to Rome (I. i. 39–49). Shakespeare had paid him a generous and unmerited compliment at the end of *Henry V*, comparing the return of the King from the victory of Agincourt to the anticipated return of Essex:

> ... But now behold
> ....
> How London doth pour out her citizens!
> The mayor and all his brethren in best sort,
> Like to the senators of th' antique Rome,
> With the plebeians swarming at their heels,
> Go forth and fetch their conquering Caesar in:
> As, by a lower but by loving likelihood,
> Were now the general of our gracious empress –
> As in good time he may – from Ireland coming,
> Bringing rebellion broached on his sword,
> How many would this peaceful city quit
> To welcome him ...

(V. Chorus, 22–34)

It is evident that Shakespeare was already contemplating the subject of his next play, and drawing parallels between the England of Elizabeth or Henry V and Caesar's Rome. In fact, the parallel was closer than he could have realised – Essex's triumphant departure had also been concluded by a thunderstorm, 'which was held an ominous portent' and Essex was eventually to be executed for treason in 1601.

It is important to be aware of the special significance of the political events of the play for Shakespeare's audience. The charge of ambition levelled against Caesar, for instance, would have carried much more weight then than now. The Elizabethans had good reason to be preoccupied with the necessity for political stability, for each man to keep his appointed place in the social hierarchy. This was regarded as the natural order of society, ordained by God according to the same pattern by which he had created the whole universe. Any departure from it was regarded as unnatural, or 'monstrous' (I. iii. 71), and was thought to be reflected by similarly 'monstrous' convulsions in the natural world and in the heavens themselves (I. iii. 62–8). The description of the portents in I. iii. continually relates these different orders of being – Cassius's threat to 'shake' the political leader (I. ii. 324) is followed immediately by the reverberations of the thunder, and the 'sway' (or 'realm') of earth 'Shakes like a thing unfirm' (I. iii. 3–4), the ocean is 'ambitious' (I. iii. 7) and the 'civil strife' on earth is mirrored in the heavens I. iii. 11). But the significance of these portents is less certain. They might represent the unnaturalness of Caesar's royal aspirations, or the unnaturalness of the murder of the head of state. As Cicero says,

> . . . men may construe things, after their fashion,
> Clean from the purpose of the things themselves.
>
> (I. iii. 34–5)

It is therefore misleading to carry the parallel between England and Rome too far; the political and moral issues are less clear-cut than in the plays concerned with English

3

history. The Elizabethans regarded monarchy as the form of government ordained by God, but the prestige of the Roman republic also stood high, although Rome had no divinely appointed king. It is possible to see Caesar as wrongfully usurping the position of king – as Montaigne saw him when he wrote that he 'sought his own glory in the ruin of his country and in the destruction of the mightiest and most flourishing commonwealth that the world will ever see' – or as the Roman equivalent of a legitimate monarch murdered by traitors – as Dante saw him when he placed Brutus and Cassius with Judas in the lowest circle of hell.

Critics of the play have differed almost as widely in their interpretation of its political themes. The play seems to invite such disagreements, but either extreme probably misrepresents it. Shakespeare had already shown in the English history plays that he was aware of the complexity of the moral issues raised by political events, and the inadequacy of one-sided views. Henry IV was a usurper, but it was better for England that he should retain power by devious political means than that Hotspur should reduce it to anarchy; Henry V may be presented as an ideal king, but in order to become the royal hero he had to repress his more generous personal feelings for Falstaff – just as Brutus feels that he must repress his personal affection for Caesar from a sense of public duty. Shakespeare could afford to be even more impartial when writing of Roman history. He puts the opposing points of view, recognising a mixture of good and evil in all his characters – and that sometimes great virtues can lead to equally great crimes. That, indeed, is the nature of tragedy.

THE SOURCE

There is a similar impartiality in Shakespeare's source for the play, Plutarch's *Lives of the Greeks and Romans*, which Sir Thomas North translated in 1579 from a French version by Jacques Amyot. It was men who interested Plutarch rather than political principles. In consequence, of all Shakespeare's sources, the *Lives* is the most dramatic in itself. Plutarch provides not only the outline of the plot, but many of the smaller incidents that give the play its life – the attempted warning by Artemidorus, the anxiety of Portia, the murder of Cinna, the quietly ominous words of the Soothsayer –

> Caesar going unto the Senate house, and speaking merrily to the Soothsayer, told him, 'The ides of March be come'; 'So be they,' softly answered the Soothsayer, 'but yet are they not past.'

Sometimes a minor character steps straight from Plutarch – one can already hear the precise tone of Decius Brutus's irony in North's translation (see note to II. ii. 93–101) – others are developed from a few hints. Of Casca all that Plutarch tells us is that he struck Caesar from behind;

> howbeit the wound was not great nor mortal, because it seemed the fear of such a devilish attempt did amaze him and take his strength from him, that he killed him not at the first blow. But Caesar, turning straight unto him, caught hold of his sword and held it hard; and they both cried out, Caesar in Latin: 'O vile traitor Casca, what dost thou?' and Casca in Greek, to his brother: 'Brother, help me.'

From this one physical action Shakespeare develops a psychological study in treachery. In the play Casca not only strikes Caesar from behind, but also attacks him verbally behind his back (I. ii. 215–76) – having been one of his most sycophantic followers to his face (I. ii. 1, 14) – while his awe-struck 'amazement' at the assassination is paralleled by his superstitious fear in the storm. His blunt forthrightness is an attempt to hide this inner weakness.

For the main actors in the drama Shakespeare expanded Plutarch's general character sketches, but he often alters details to make the characters more coherent. While Plutarch attributes Brutus's sleeplessness to his anxiety about the success of the plot, and his estrangement from Cassius to their rivalry for the post of praetor, Shakespeare ascribes both to Brutus's anxiety about the condition of Rome, thus deepening his character and strengthening his motivation for joining the conspiracy by implying that Cassius's spiteful attack on Caesar was only a contributory factor.

For many of the most dramatic scenes, such as III. ii, Plutarch provided little guidance. The speeches of Brutus and Antony to the crowd are almost entirely Shakespeare's invention, although he modelled them on Plutarch's description of their styles of rhetoric. Brutus

> counterfeited that brief, compendious manner of speech of the Lacedaemonians; as, when the war was begun, he wrote unto the Pergamenians in this sort: 'I understand you have given Dolabella money: if you have done it willingly, you confess you have offended me; if against your wills, show it then by giving me willingly.' Another time again unto the Samians: 'Your councils be long, your doings be slow, consider the end.'

From the balanced sentences of these examples Shakespeare constructed a 'brief, compendious' and elaborately-patterned oration. For Antony's speech Plutarch provided some guidance on the content and manner (see notes to III. ii. 77–260, 181–7), and its flamboyance may have been suggested by his comment that Antony 'used a manner of phrase in his speech called Asiatic, which . . . was much like to his manners and life; for it was full of ostentation, foolish knavery, and vain ambition', but its cunning and moving eloquence are Shakespeare's own. So too are the individual responses of the crowd in this scene, and in the first two scenes of the play. They are modelled on the lower-class characters of the English history plays, with their cheerful impertinence (I. i. 10–33), their sententiousness (III. ii. 73–4), their truculance (III. ii. 72), their sentimentality (I. ii. 272-6; III. ii. 119), their irrationality (III. ii. 54-5), and their ruthless brutality (III. iii).

STRUCTURE

The crowd is one of the main forces in the drama, the underlying power that determines the outcome as it is worked on by the leading characters. That is the reason, as Bradley pointed out,[1] why we are introduced to it in the first scene. At first it appears as a collection of individuals – the cobbler is a character in his own right – but there are already ominous signs of its weakness for hero-worship and its readiness to be swayed by emotional rhetoric. Throughout the scenes that follow, the crowd is never far from the minds of the leading characters, erupting on to the stage whenever Caesar enters in public, rumbling threateningly in the distance to give point to Cassius's invective against Caesar, described sardonically by Casca, gathering as a background to the anxieties of Portia and the Soothsayer, and finally transformed into a mindless mob by the speech of Antony. The first movement of the play closes as it began, with the crowd. Their brutal cross-questioning of Cinna is an ironic reversal of Marullus's arrogant interrogation of the cobbler in the first scene, and their cheerful humour recurs in a warped, distorted form in the black comedy of Cinna's murder.

Shakespeare gives further unity to the action by telescoping the historical sequence of events. Caesar's triumph, which actually took place in October, 45 B.C., is combined with the Lupercalia of the following February, and is made the occasion of the Soothsayer's first warning; Antony's speech follows immediately after that of Brutus, instead of two days later; the triumvirate meet on the same day, although Octavius did not in fact arrive in Rome for several weeks, and was hostile to Antony for over a year before joining with him and Lepidus in July 43; the two battles of Philippi were not fought until late in the following

[1] A. C. Bradley, *Shakespearian Tragedy* (Macmillan, 1904).

year, and Shakespeare truncates the campaign radically – the 'second fight' (V. iii. 110) actually took place twenty-days after the first. In the earlier acts he carries this process further, working on two different time-scales. The first line of I. iii. suggests that the storm occurs on the night of the Lupercalia, but by lines 36–8 it is already the eve of the ides of March, and the last two lines link this scene directly with the next, where the date is again emphasised. On the other hand, Brutus's soliloquy must indicate that an extended period of time has passed since Cassius incited him to turn against Caesar (II. i. 61–2). In the theatre an audience would have no opportunity to compare these two time-scales; we gain a simultaneous impression of Brutus's lengthy brooding on the conspiracy and of events moving inexorably towards the climax.

As the hour of the murder approaches, the passage of time is charted with still greater precision and the tempo increases. Act Two opens with Brutus concerned to know the time, and the apparently inconsequential argument between the conspirators about the position of the east (II. i. 101–11) points to the dawn as a symbol of their hopes for the following day. They separate at three o'clock and arrange to meet at eight (II. i. 192, 213), giving a sinister note to Caesar's enquiry about the time and Brutus's reply (II. ii. 114). The brief scenes with Artemidorus and Portia further increase the tension by temporarily holding up the action while still emphasising the passage of time – by II. iv. 23 it is nine o'clock – and the gathering of the crowd. They also introduce the possibility that the conspiracy will be betrayed, by Artemidorus's warning or by Portia's agitation, which is itself communicated to the audience. In the Senate this pattern of urgent forward movement and anxious restraint is further concentrated. The ominous date is announced in the first line and the conspirators press forward; as they are checked briefly by Artemidorus, by the intervention of Popilius Lena, and by Caesar's increasingly garrulous rhetoric, so they become more importunate (III. i. 49–

57) and the exchange briefer (III. i. 74-5) in a final acceleration to the murder.

The brief scenes that precede the assassination have a further purpose in balancing the sympathies of the audience between the fears of Artemidorus for Caesar and those of Portia for Brutus. This pairing of scenes or episodes is characteristic of the structure of the play. Antony's speech is juxtaposed to that of Brutus, the savage murder of Cinna is followed by the cold-blooded planning of judicial murders by the triumvirs, their equally cold rivalry – Antony's cynical dismissal of Lepidus (IV. i. 12-40) and Octavius's assertion of his authority over Antony (V. i. 16-20) – frames the hotblooded quarrel between Brutus and Cassius and their moving reconciliation. Most revealing of all are the parallel scenes between Brutus and Portia and between Caesar and Calphurnia. Calphurnia has been frightened out of her submissiveness into a querulous attack on Caesar. There is no sense of intimacy between them. Caesar assumes his most grandiose manner, and the nearest he comes to sympathy is the rather patronising indulgence with which he agrees to humour her (II. ii. 55-6), before Decius Brutus persuades him to dismiss her fears with equally patronising contempt (II. ii. 105-7). Portia's quiet intrusion into Brutus's thoughts contrasts with Calphurnia's petulant outburst. Between Brutus and Portia there is a sense of mutual respect throughout. Calphurnia's speeches have a nervously staccato quality and she breaks in when it would have been better to remain silent (II. ii 65); Portia's have a smooth rhythmical persistence as she quietly emphasises the evidence she has accumulated – she produces her trump-card with no special emphasis (II. i. 275-8) – and counters Brutus's excuses with gentle irony (II. i. 258-67), seeking only to share his troubles and demonstrating her right to do so.

The play becomes a close-knit pattern of significantly related scenes, which provides its own commentary on the major characters and events. And the balance is not always tilted in favour of Brutus's party; the hysteria of their self-congratulatory heroics after they have killed one unprepared man (III. i. 111–21) is effectively punctured by the nobility of Antony's grief and his tributes to the genuinely heroic character of the man they have murdered.

CAESAR

There is a sense of Caesar's greatness throughout the play. To Brutus he is never less than 'the foremost man of all this world' (IV. iii. 22), and it is Cassius who, at the height of his invective against Caesar, produces one of the most memorable images of him as superman:

> Why man, he doth bestride the narrow world
> Like a Colossus . . .
>
> (I. ii. 135–6)

As Antony remarks ironically when he thinks Cassius is about to object to his praise of Caesar,

> The enemies of Caesar shall say this;
> Then, in a friend, it is cold modesty.
>
> (III. i. 212–13)

Yet we learn of his greatness from what others say of him rather than from what he says or does himself. At times, indeed, he seems even before his death to be the 'ruins' of the noblest man that 'ever lived in the tide of times' (III. i. 256–7). His nobility has degenerated into arrogance. He certainly wishes to be crowned and woos the crowd like a popular demogogue (I. ii. 221–76). He already behaves like an autocrat, speaking of 'Caesar and his senate' (III. i. 32), as if the senators were merely ministers appointed by him, and displaying his contempt for them openly to Decius Brutus:

> Have I in conquest stretched mine arm so far
> To be afeard to tell greybeards the truth?
>
> (II. ii. 66–7)

The only justification his actions need is that they are his will (II. ii. 71–2).

This is the initial impression we are given of him. At his first entrance his orders are brief and peremptory. The distinguished Romans who attend him are there only to call for silence when he speaks, or to carry out his instructions – 'When Caesar says, "Do this," it is performed' (I. ii. 10). Even his wife does not accompany him, but has to be summoned when required, and he shows little consideration for her feelings when he refers to her sterility in public – a detail that Shakespeare added to Plutarch's account. The impression is even more striking when he returns from the ceremonies in the Forum: because his mood has changed 'all the rest look like a chidden train' (I. ii. 184), as if dependent on a tyrant's whim. Shakespeare seems determined to stress his autocracy; when Flavius and Marullus are 'put to silence' (I. ii. 287) an audience is likely to assume that this is a euphemism for 'put to death', although in Plutarch they are merely dismissed from their offices.

There are flashes of those qualities that enabled him to rise to power, but the effect of most of these is ambiguous. His gracious welcome of the conspirators on the morning of the ideas of March (II. ii. 108–27) seems to express a genuine friendship, but there is a touch of the condescending affability of the tyrant, airily tossing a word to each, 'Now, Cinna; now, Metellus; what, Trebonius' (II. ii. 120). His former shrewdness is evident in his assessment of Cassius (I. ii. 192–210), yet he spoils the effect by his self-conscious protest that he does not fear him, 'for always I am Caesar' (I. ii. 212). This practice of referring to himself in the third person – even in private (II. ii. 10, 28) – is symptomatic of his arrogance. He contemplates himself as he hopes others see him, his public image; he must always consider what is expected of the bearer of the name of Caesar. Thus, while he is prepared to deceive the Senate with a lying excuse when Antony is to be his messenger, he changes his mind when Decius Brutus knows it to be untrue

– 'Shall Caesar send a lie?' (II. ii. 55–6, 65). One of his finest moments comes when he refuses to read Artemidorus's warning letter – 'What touches us ourself shall be last served' (III. i. 8). This instance is important since Shakespeare again departs from Plutarch, who says merely that Caesar attempted to read the warning but was prevented by the number of people greeting him. The change adds a touch of genuine nobility before the murder. Yet the suspicion that he may be fostering his public image shadows the moment of greatness, and his use of the royal plural – 'us ourself' – suggests that he was not unaware of the regal gesture he was making.

Shakespeare's Caesar is a study of the ambiguities of political greatness. He deliberately contrasts Caesar's human frailties with the public image that he cultivates. His claim to an almost god-like immunity from fear is immediately followed by a reference to his deafness (I. ii. 213) – which was another addition by Shakespeare. Similarly, the 'falling sickness' – which Plutarch mentions elsewhere – attacks Caesar in the play at the height of his triumph (I. ii. 253–5).

Caesar's attitude to the predictions of his death is equally ambiguous. He listens attentively to the Soothsayer, but dismisses him as a dreamer (I. ii. 12–24); yet he still remembers the warning, if only to ignore it (III. i. 1). He is sufficiently impressed by the storm to consult the augurers, yet he chooses to give their omen a favourable interpretation (II. ii. 5–6, 38–43). It has been said that he is a prey to superstition, chiefly on the evidence of Cassius (II. i. 195–8), but Cassius is clearly an unreliable witness to Caesar's character. It is true that he hopes that the ceremonies of Lupercalia will cure Calphurnia of barrenness, but it can be argued that this is a mark of piety and respect for traditional wisdom (I. ii. 7) rather than superstition. It might also be pointed out that belief in omens is amply justified by the events of the play, and that Cassius himself changes his mind about them (V. i. 77–9).

Caesar's fault is the reverse, an excessive self-confidence; it is when his 'wisdom is consumed in confidence' (II. ii. 49) that 'Security gives way to conspiracy' (II. iii. 7–8). He has come so to identify himself with his public image that he talks boastful nonsense:

> . . . . Danger knows full well
> That Caesar is more dangerous than he.
>
> (II. ii. 44–5)

More dangerously, it lays him open to flattery. It is his complacent acceptance of Decius Brutus's interpretation of Calphurnia's dream – which attributes to him mystical, semi-divine powers – as well as his desire for the crown and his fear of mockery, that persuades him to go to the Senate. He resembles those heroes of Greek tragedy whose besetting sin is hubris, the blasphemous pride that makes a man believe he has risen above humanity, and that the gods punish with destruction. It is also with the irony of Greek tragedy that his hubris reaches a climax immediately before his murder. He distinguishes himself from 'ordinary men' and claims a god-like 'constancy' and immunity from error (III. i. 37, 47–8, 60–74) at the very moment that his mere humanity is to be demonstrated.

But it is also a truly noble humanity that is revealed at his murder. With his tragic cry, 'Et tu, Brute? Then fall, Caesar!' it is as if his genuine greatness of soul has been released from the human frailties that have distorted it into arrogance. From this point all the emphasis is on his magnanimity and achievements – 'all thy conquests, glories, triumphs, spoils' (III. i. 149). This is the Caesar that sends the crowd raging after the conspirators, and whose spirit, 'ranging for revenge' (III. i. 270), dominates the rest of the play, appearing twice as a ghost to Brutus (V. v. 17–20), and haunting the conspirators with a sense of disillusionment until it is appeased by their deaths (V. iii. 45–6, 94–6; V. v. 50–1).

BRUTUS

Caesar's last cry, with its accusation of – and lament for – the betrayal of friendship, sums up the tragedy of Brutus; for if the play has a tragic hero it is Brutus. He is a hero on the pattern described by Aristotle, a man of great virtues but with one fatal flaw that leads to his destruction. As with Caesar, the most convincing testimony to his virtues is supplied by his enemy – he is 'the noblest Roman of them all' (V. v. 68).

His character is an elaboration from Plutarch's brief general description:

> having framed his manners of life by the rules of virtue and study of philosophy, and having employed his wit, which was gentle and constant, in attempting of great things, methinks he was rightly made and framed unto virtue.

The philosophy he studies is Stoicism, the fundamental principle of which is that nothing is of value except virtue. The Stoic therefore disciplines himself both to despise worldly pleasures and to ignore the calamities that fortune may bring. Secure in his own virtue, he can resign himself to divine providence, accepting whatever it sends him with equanimity. There can be no need for suicide (see V. i. 101–8); it is an impious attempt to avoid the fate ordained by the gods, and a sign of weakness in admitting that external events can have power over a man; all that matters is his own virtue. One sees the Stoic in Brutus's devotion to virtue, honour, and his duty to Rome, in the calm fortitude with which he accepts Portia's death or keeps a grip on himself when Popilius Lena seems about to betray the plot to Caesar (III. i. 13–24), in his measured, rational reply to Cassius's invective against Caesar (I. ii. 162–75) and in his fatal belief that the crowd will be equally responsive to reason.

Brutus's faults are as much a part of his Stoicism as his virtues. In seeking to free a man from human frailties it is liable to be an unrealistic creed, encouraging its adherents to have excessive confidence in themselves. Brutus's self-confidence is not, like Caesar's, in the power of his personality, but in the purity of his motives and rightness of his judgements. Like Caesar, he is equally a victim of his own public image. The high esteem in which he is held blinds him to his human fallibility. He does not really know himself,

> .... for the eye sees not itself
> But by reflection, by some other things.
>
> (I. ii. 52–3)

Cassius offers to act as his 'mirror', to show him himself, but instead shows him his external reputation in Rome (I. ii. 58–62) and what is expected of him as the supposed descendant of Lucius Junius Brutus:

> There was a Brutus once that would have brooked
> Th' eternal devil to keep his state in Rome
> As easily as a king.
>
> (I. ii. 159–61)

This is what is expected of 'a Brutus', and Brutus is almost as prone as Caesar to speak of himself in the third person, dwelling on the virtues enshrined in that name (I. ii. 172; III. ii. 20–1; IV. iii. 79; V. ii. 112). One of his chief motives for joining the conspiracy is the belief that Rome expects it of him. His final decision follows immediately after his receipt of the letters forged by Cassius (II. i. 56–8), and the scene ends with the tribute of Caius Ligarius; 'it sufficeth/That Brutus leads me on'. His name is enough – just as Caesar expected his will to be sufficient justification. There is a disturbing parallel between the semi-divine powers attributed to Caesar by Decius Brutus and the 'miraculous' power of healing that Ligarius ascribes to Brutus. His idealised image of himself makes Brutus also susceptible to flattery.

Thus he assumes the leadership of the conspiracy as an

unquestioned right, and imposes his will on his colleagues as absolutely as Caesar imposes his on Rome. One cannot but admire the high ideals he expresses, and be exasperated by the complacency with which he expresses them. A producer is free to choose which of these feelings should predominate; but Shakespeare surely intended an ironic comment when he altered the reason that Plutarch gives for the exclusion of Cicero from the conspiracy and makes Brutus object that

> . . . he will never follow any thing
> That other men begin.

(II. i. 151-2)

The particular errors he makes also follow from this lofty detachment from 'ordinary men'. He spares Antony not only to avoid unnecessary bloodshed, but because he despises a man given 'To sports, to wildness, and much company' (II. i. 186-9; see also I. ii. 28-9), and he allows Antony to speak at Caesar's funeral because he overestimates the power of his own oratory and the influence on the crowd of appeals to reason and, significantly, of his own reputation (III. i. 236-7; III. ii. 15-18). Brutus shows them the image of himself, Antony shows them the corpse of Caesar.

But perhaps his fundamental error is his decision to join the conspiracy. There has been considerable difference of opinion about this. Brutus can be seen as the champion of freedom against tyranny, or as the mistaken idealist who murders not only his friend but the one man who could impose stable and responsible rule on Rome. There is ample evidence in the play of Caesar's autocratic behaviour, but little of actual acts of tyranny, apart from the uncertain fate of the tribunes. Brutus, himself, has not noticed any:

> . . . to speak truth of Caesar,
> I have not known when his affections swayed
> More than his reason.

(II. i. 19-21)

Both in this soliloquy and in his earlier reply to Cassius (I. ii. 174–5) he refers only to possible future evils. He condemns Caesar not for what he has done but for what he might do – 'Then lest he may, prevent' (II. i. 28). His fear that the crowning of Caesar 'might change his nature' (II. i. 13) has often been justified by Lord Acton's maxim that 'power tends to corrupt, and absolute power corrupts absolutely'. This is the sort of theoretical generalisation that would appeal to Brutus, but it overlooks the fact that Caesar already enjoys almost regal power and, according to Brutus, has not been corrupted. It is the name of king to which he objects. He has already decided at the beginning of the soliloquy that 'It must be by his death', and now is merely finding reasons to justify the decision:

> . . . since the quarrel
> Will bear no colour for the thing he is,
> Fashion it thus . . .
>
> (II. i. 28–30)

– the last phrase suggests contrivance, even casuistry.

His attempt to pursue an abstract ideal amidst political realities that he does not fully understand involves him in continual self-contradictions. His fastidious disgust at the external deception required by conspiracy leads him to urge a still more insidious deceit –

> . . . Seek none, conspiracy;
> Hide it in smiles and affability . . .
>
> (II. i. 81–2)

He insists on the purity of their motives, yet welcomes Caius Ligarius to the plot because he has a grudge against Caesar (II. i. 215–20). His self-righteousness prevents him from seeing the contradictions in his attitude to the means by which Cassius raises money (see note to IV. iii. 71). He attempts to transform the murder into a ritual sacrifice (II. i. 166–8), and to demonstrate this by the ritual washing in Caesar's blood (III. i. 105–10), but the very action by which he seeks to ennoble the deed leaves them looking all the more like 'butchers' (III. i. 158, 184, 198), as he himself admits (III. i. 165–8). His idealised view of the assassination cannot compete with the physical reality, and the corpse of Caesar remains on stage for the greater part of two scenes as a reminder of the brutality of murder. His wish that they might 'come by Caesar's spirit' without dismembering Caesar (II. i. 169–70) is ironically reversed: they are left with the 'dismembered' body while the tyranny that Brutus identifies with the spirit of Caesar is released.

There is no sign that Brutus ever recognises that he might have been wrong. In the quarrel scene he is still insisting on the nobility of their deed, yet there is a mood of weary fatalism through the last two acts, and it is his wish to be rid of the whole business (V. i. 123–6) that prompts his final error of staking their cause on a single battle. He recognises the appearance of Caesar's ghost as a sign of failure, if not of guilt (V. v. 17–20) and acknowledges the fitness of his death (V. v. 50–51).

The tragedy of Brutus's failure in public affairs is heightened by the attractiveness of his private life, in his love for Portia, his consideration for his attendants (IV. iii. 246–50), and his affectionate sympathy for Lucius (II. i. 229–33; IV. iii. 240–1, 252–72). The one achievement with which he consoles himself at the end of the play is in the sphere of personal relationships:

> My heart doth joy that yet in all my life
> I found no man but he was true to me.
>
> (V. v. 34–5)

His emotions are the stronger for being so sternly repressed. They are least attractive when they find expression in the moral ferocity with which he attacks Cassius in their quarrel, but their reconciliation is the all the more moving. His deeper feelings have to be forced from him, as Portia's affectionate persistence at last wrings out his declaration of love and trust (II. i. 288–90, 302–3).

CASSIUS AND ANTONY

It might have been better for Brutus to trust his emotions rather than his reason, instead of allowing an abstract moral ideal to overcome his love for Caesar. In this respect he has been compared unfavourably with Cassius and Antony, both of whom are ultimately governed by their emotions. In the most penetrating summary of Cassius's character – that by Caesar himself (I. ii. 192–210) – he is contrasted with Antony, but Cassius knows that Antony is also a 'shrewd contriver' (II. i. 158), and the two have much in common. In contrast to Brutus's stoicism, both are Epicureans in their different ways. Epicurus had sought to release men from the supernatural fears that hinder the enjoyment of the pleasures of life by denying that the gods concern themselves with human affairs. Antony is an Epicurean in the popular sense (I. ii. 28–9, 203–4; II. i. 188–9; V. i. 62); Cassius is the philosophical Epicurean, showing his contempt for supposed supernatural warnings (I. iii. 43–52) and asserting that men are masters of their own fate (I. ii. 139–41).

While Brutus acts on principle, Cassius and Antony are Epicureans in their opportunism and lack of moral scruple. As Antony watches the crowd and adjusts his oratory to their response, so Cassius adapts his approach to the man he is addressing. With the superstitious Casca he affects a belief in omens so that he can interpret them to suit his own purpose (I. iii. 62–78); with Brutus his approach is more philosophical, posing a question that will appeal to his speculative mind (I. ii. 51). He circles round his real subject, looking for an opening, picking up Brutus's words and twisting them to his own purpose (I. ii. 92), and seizing on the opportunity offered by Brutus's reaction to the crowd (I. ii. 80, 135). Both of them exploit their own emotions, Antony playing on the feelings of the crowd by a demonstration of his own grief (III. ii. 109–11), and Cassius seeking to infect Brutus with his own hatred of Caesar and to arouse the 'quick mettle' of Casca by a flamboyant display of his own recklessness (I. iii. 89–115). Cassius is given to making theatrical gestures. On three occasions he declares his immediate readiness to face death (I. iii. 89–100; III. i. 20–2; IV. iii. 100–7), and it is characteristically he who sees the murder of Caesar in terms of the theatre (III. i. 111–13).

Both Cassius and Antony might have qualified to be the villains of the play. Plutarch describes Cassius as a 'hot, choleric and cruel man'

> . . . hating Caesar privately more than he did the tyranny openly, he incensed Brutus against him. It is also reported that Brutus could evil away with the tyranny, and that Cassius hated the tyrant, making many complaints for the injuries he had done him.

Thus in the play, when Brutus speaks of honour, Cassius sees it only in terms of his personal inferiority to Caesar (I. ii. 90–131), and his spite is evident in his use of any circumstance to denigrate Caesar (I. ii. 100–31). He sometimes seems equally unscrupulous in his attitude to Brutus. He is prepared to deceive him with fabricated letters (I. ii. 317–22), and at the start of this soliloquy appears at first sight to be gloating over his success in manipulating his noble friend. Yet there is a strange ambiguity here (see note to I. ii. 317). Cassius might be congratulating himself on his skill in working on Brutus's 'honourable mettle', or he might be reflecting on the danger that even the noble Brutus might be 'seduced' by Caesar's love. The second interpretation is certainly more consistent with the respect that he shows Brutus as leader of the conspiracy. There is an ironic pathos in the way he must watch his plans being wrecked by the man whose leadership he had worked so hard to obtain; yet only once does he remind Brutus of his mistakes (V. i. 45–7). After the assassination he becomes an increasingly sympathetic character, especially in the quarrel scene; he blurts out his complaint with characteristic impetuosity (IV. ii. 37), but his anger is soon over, in contrast to Brutus's unrelenting moral hardness. Personal details – that it is his birthday (V. i. 72), and that he inherited his 'rash humour' from his mother (IV. iii. 120) – help to make him more human. He too becomes oppressed with a sense of fate (V. i. 71–89; V. iii. 23–5), and his death – caused by that same impetuous rashness – is invested with a nobility that equals that of Brutus.

The contrary extremes of character are even more marked in Antony. He is more unscrupulous than Cassius – the scene in which he bargains over the proscriptions with his fellow triumvirs, plans to deprive the plebeians of Caesar's legacies, and dismisses Lepidus 'as a property', is completely devoid of any generous feelings – yet his love for Caesar and his response to his death have a generosity and gallantry unrivalled in the play. He is the amateur virtuoso in politics. He seems careless on his first appearance, casually dismissing Cassius as a danger (I. ii. 196–7), but his apparent carelessness gives him a poise and flexibility that enables him to run rings round the conspirators, while his convivial life has taught him how to speak to the common people on their own level, presenting himself as a fellow mourner and trading on his supposed lack of subtlety (III. ii. 223–30). From the moment he enters after the murder of Caesar he is master of the situation, with the cool assurance of the hero of a Western entering a bar crowded with his enemies. To disclaim his love for Caesar would deceive nobody, but he knows Brutus well enough to realise that a frank expression of his grief and the offer of his own life is the most certain way of ensuring his safety. The calm, supple rhythm of his speech and the effortless ease with which he turns aside possible threats suggest the technique of a skilful games player, and his veiled irony reveals a secret enjoyment of his skill. But the emotion is none the less genuine, and when he is alone his intense love for Caesar is combined with a fierce ruthlessness in his prophecy of revenge. In the scenes that follow it is the ruthlessness that is more apparent, but his nobility emerges again at the end of the play with his reception of the captured Lucilius (V. iv. 26–9) and his generous tribute to Brutus.

ROME

Ultimately, one might say, they are all noble Romans. Even Casca can refer proudly to the virtues epitomised by his name:

> You speak to Casca, and to such a man
> That is no fleering tell-tale.
>
> (I. iii. 116–17)

This sense of the Roman character and of the Roman inheritance unifies the play. The name that resounds most frequently is that of Rome itself; the adjective 'Roman' is sufficient to identify the ideals to which all the characters subscribe, and when even Brutus's Stoic principles conflict with his Roman sense of honour, it is Roman honour that wins (V. i. 111–13).

Julius Caesar is a very Roman play. Its structure has a classical strength and simplicity, rising like a great arch to the twin climaxes of the assassination and Antony's speech and descending with smooth inevitability to the suicides of Cassius and Brutus. Its style is elevated and rhetorical, appropriate to the nobility and public nature of its theme. While the rhetoric is varied according to the character of the speaker – as the balanced fluency of Antony differs from the stabbing staccato of Cassius – the rhetorical form gives them all a common dignity. It invests even the crowd through the full, unhurried rhythms of Marullus's description of them:

> ... Many a time and oft
> Have you climbed up to walls and battlements,
> To towers and windows, yea, to chimney-tops ...
>
> (I. i. 39–41)

There is little of the suggestive imagery or half-articulated thoughts that take us deeply into the mind of a Hamlet or a

Lear; its statements are explicit and fully formed for public communication.

When the rhetoric is most complex, as in Brutus's speech to the crowd, the language is most simple and direct. *Julius Caesar* is not only a Roman, but also a masculine play. The intense emotions are those between men: the love of Brutus and Antony for Caesar, the mutual love of Brutus and Cassius, the devotion of Brutus's attendants to him, and of Lucilius to Cassius, the tenderness of Brutus for Lucius – even Artemidorus signs his letter to Caesar, 'Thy lover'. It is noticeable that the only characteristic referred to as distinctively feminine is weakness (I. iii. 84; II. i. 122; II. iv. 8) – when Portia appeals to Brutus's love it is by demonstrating her masculine virtues, to show that she is 'Cato's daughter' (II. i. 295–302). The strongest emotional statements tend to be brief and direct –

> You are my true and honourable wife,
> As dear to me as are the ruddy drops
> That visit my sad heart.
>
> (II. i. 288–90)

> Do you confess so much? Give me your hand.
>
> (IV. iii. 117)

> Et tu, Brute? Then fall, Caesar!
>
> (III. i. 77)

– culminating in Brutus's Stoical response to the news of Portia's death.

The imagery has a similar Roman austerity. Typical is the neat pun on 'mettle' and 'metal' that runs through the play (I. i. 63; I. ii. 298, 311; II. i. 134) and is associated with the sharpening and working of metals (I. ii. 311; II. i. 61, 210; III. i. 175; V. iii. 75–8) – in contrast to the 'bluntness' of Casca (I. ii. 297) and the pretended bluntness of Antony (III. ii. 225). The use of steel to strike a spark from flint (I. ii. 176–7; II. i. 120–1; IV. iii. 111–13) links this imagery with the many references to fire in the play – the fiery portents, the fire of pity (III. i. 171), Ligarius's heart 'new-fired' (II. i. 332), Cicero's 'fiery eyes' (I. ii. 186) and Antony's eyes 'red as fire with weeping' (III. ii. 119), the fire with which the mob burns the conspirators' houses and the fire that Portia swallows. This pattern of imagery suggests the spirit and hardness of the Roman character – 'those sparks of life/That should be in a Roman' (I. iii. 57–8) – and is further associated with metaphors from horse-manship, especially the firm control of a spirited horse (I. ii. 35–6; IV. i. 29–35; IV. ii. 23–7), from hunting (II. i. 173–4; III. i. 204–10), falconry (I. i. 74–7; II. i. 118) and bear-baiting (IV. i. 48–9; IV. iii. 28).

But the most powerful images arise from the action itself, from the bloodstained body of Caesar about which the action turns. The inheritance of Roman virtues is identified with Roman blood: Rome has 'lost the breed of noble bloods' (I. ii. 151), each drop of the conspirators' blood would be guilty of bastardy if they betrayed their cause (II. i. 136–40), and Caesar's – 'the most noble blood of all this world' – would be 'rebel blood' if he were to be moved by flattery (III. i. 40). The play is full of images of blood; it is drizzled on the Capitol (II. ii. 21), it is the signal for battle (V. i. 14) and it provides a noble shroud for Cassius (V. iii. 62). The blood of Caesar becomes the central symbol of the play, the ambiguity of its interpretation reflecting the ambiguity of our attitude to his assassination. It is a sign both of the nobility of the deed (III. i. 105–7) and of its brutality (III. i. 165–8). This pattern of symbolism grows from Plutarch's simple statement that in the confusion of the murder the conspirators wounded each other, 'every man of them bloodied', while the mystical character of the blood may have been suggested by North's fortunate mis-translation in making Pompey's statue bleed sympathetic-ally while the murder was being committed – a phenomenon that is also open to diverse interpretations (see note to III. ii. 196). Shakespeare extends the complex significance of blood by making it the subject of Calphurnia's dream and

Decius's interpretation of it. In ambiguous fulfilment of both the dream and the interpretation, the conspirators wash their hands in Caesar's blood (III. i. 105–10) and the crowd would dip their napkins in it (III. ii. 137): Brutus sees it as symbolising the revival of Roman liberty; Antony uses it to revive the spirit of Caesarism.

The whole play is also encompassed by the symbolism of light and darkness. The conspirators' meetings are at night (I. iii; II. i; IV. iii), which is associated with unnatural terrors and disease (II. i. 235–6, 261–7; V. iii. 64) and signifies the darkness from which they would liberate Rome, the deceitful concealment that conspiracy entails (II. i. 77–81, 277–8), and perhaps their blindness to political realities – Cassius's sight was 'ever-thick' (V. iii. 21). The conflict in Brutus's mind is compared to a 'hideous dream' (II. i. 65) which becomes a supernatural reality when the ghost enters at Sardis. His inability to sleep is contrasted with the innocent slumber of Lucius (II. i. 229–33; IV. iii. 227–8, 240–1, 254–72), who, with his tapers, brings a glow of light into the tragic darkness (II. i. 7–8; IV. iii. 157) – his name means 'light'. In II. i. the conspirators look towards the dawn (lines 101–11) and the progress towards the day of action is carefully mapped out (see p. 8); but in IV. iii. it is the growing darkness of which we are aware – 'The deep of night is crept upon our talk' (IV. iii. 226). At Philippi their fortunes sink with the setting sun, which provides a last radiance to illuminate the nobility of their deaths – the sunlight itself becoming identified with blood:

> . . . O setting sun,
> As in thy red rays thou dost sink tonight,
> So in his red blood Cassius' day is set.
> The sun of Rome is set. Our day is gone . . .
>
> (V. iii. 60–3)

While our conflicting sympathies are concentrated in the symbolism of Caesar's blood, this natural progress from darkness through day to darkness again expresses the inevitable defeat of the conspiracy – as Brutus says with Stoic fortitude:

> Night hangs upon mine eyes; my bones would rest,
> That have but laboured to attain this hour.
>
> (V. v. 41–2)

HISTORICAL NOTE

The play opens after the victory of Julius Caesar over Gnaeus and Sextus, the sons of Pompey, at the battle of Munda in 45 BC. In 60 BC Caesar, Pompey and Crassus had formed the first 'triumvirate' (ruling group of three men), governing Rome largely in defiance of the Senate, but while Caesar was occupied in the conquest of Gaul, Crassus had been killed fighting the Parthians – the campaign in which Cassius had captured Pindarus (V. iii. 37) – and Pompey had begun to intrigue against him, posing as the champion of the Senate. In 49 BC Caesar crossed the Rubicon with his legions, and in the civil war that followed, Pompey was defeated at the battle of Pharsalus (48 BC) and subsequently murdered when he fled to Egypt. Brutus and Cassius both fought on Pompey's side but Caesar not only pardoned Brutus and made him a close friend, but also granted his request that Cassius should be allowed to return to Rome. With the defeat of Pompey's sons, all opposition to Caesar seemed to be crushed. Individual members of the senatorial party were still antagonistic, but there was little popular opposition to the growth of his power – the tribunes, whose office had originally been created to uphold the rights of the common people, are represented in the play as adherents of Pompey rather than as defenders of liberty. He had been made 'dictator' (a title that did not then have its modern obloquy) and given the right to appoint all officers of state; honours were heaped on him, and a statue erected in the Capitol with the inscription 'to the demi-god'. As he had no legitimate son, he had adopted his great-nephew Octavius as his heir.

JULIUS CAESAR

THE CHARACTERS

JULIUS CAESAR
OCTAVIUS CAESAR
MARK ANTONY
M. AEMILIUS LEPIDUS } triumvirs after the death of Julius Caesar

CICERO
PUBLIUS
POPILIUS LENA } senators

MARCUS BRUTUS
CASSIUS
CASCA
TREBONIUS
LIGARIUS
DECIUS BRUTUS
METELLUS CIMBER
CINNA } conspirators against Julius Caesar

FLAVIUS and MARULLUS, tribunes
ARTEMIDORUS, a teacher of rhetoric
A SOOTHSAYER
CINNA, a poet
A POET
LUCILIUS, TITINIUS, MESSALA, YOUNG CATO, VOLUMNIUS, friends to Brutus and Cassius
VARRO, CLITUS, CLAUDIUS, STRATO, LUCIUS, DARDANIUS, FLAVIUS, LABEO, servants or officers to Brutus
PINDARUS, servant to Cassius
CALPHURNIA, wife to Caesar
PORTIA, wife to Brutus

Senators, Citizens, Guards, Attendants, Soldiers

ACT ONE, scene 1

Groups of commoners enter in a cheerful mood, meeting the tribunes.

[3] Being mechanical   *As you are manual workers*

[4–5] sign ... profession   *the clothes and tools appropriate to your occupation. There were no statutes about workmen's dress in either Rome or Elizabethan England; Flavius means only that on a working day they should be equipped for work.*

[10] in respect of   *in comparison to*

[11] a cobbler   *punning on the two meanings of 'cobbler' – 'shoe-mender' and 'clumsy workman'*

[12] directly   *plainly, without punning*

[13] use   *practise*

[15] soles   *punning on 'soles' (of shoes) and 'souls' – both words were spelt 'soul' in the First Folio*

[16] What trade ... trade?   *This speech is given to Flavius in the Folio, but it is clearly part of the interchange between Marullus and the citizen, and has his peremptory tone.*

naughty knave   *worthless fellow. 'Naught' means 'good for nothing'.*

[17–18] out ... out   *The citizen continues to pun. The first 'out' means 'angry' (as in 'fall out with') – in which case 'mend you' means 'improve your character', as Marullus understands it – but it could also mean 'out at heel' (i.e. 'if your shoes need mending').*

[22–3] all ... awl   *This is another pun; an awl is a tool for boring holes in leather.*

[23–4] meddle ... women's matters   *I don't interfere with either the business of merchants or the affairs of women. It sounds as if there is a hidden allusion here, which may be to Thomas Dekker's* The Shoemakers' Holiday, *written to celebrate the trade of shoe-making, and acted in 1599. Its hero, Simon Eyre, grew rich by trading rather than by shoemaking, and helped solve the romantic problems of the play's two heroines.*

[24] withal   *a complex pun – 'withal' means 'yet', 'at the same time', but it can also be read as 'with all' ('but I meddle with all') and 'with awl' (continuing the pun of ll. 22–3). These different meanings call for different punctuation, but an actor could convey the ambiguity by a significant pause after the word.*

[26] recover   *both 'repair' (shoes) and 'restore to health'*

[26–7] As proper ... leather   *a proverbial saying – 'as good a man as ever walked in shoes'. 'Neat' is a term for cattle.*

ACT ONE

Scene 1. *Enter* FLAVIUS, MARULLUS *and certain* CITIZENS
over the stage

FLAVIUS Hence! home, you idle creatures, get you
home.
Is this a holiday? What, know you not,
Being mechanical, you ought not walk
Upon a labouring day without the sign
Of your profession? Speak, what trade art
thou?

FIRST CITIZEN Why, sir, a carpenter.

MARULLUS Where is thy leather apron and thy rule?
What dost thou with thy best apparel on?
You, sir, what trade are you?

SECOND CITIZEN Truly, sir, in respect of a fine work-   10
man, I, am but, as you would say, a cobbler.

MARULLUS But what trade art thou? Answer me
directly.

SECOND CITIZEN A trade, sir, that I hope I may use
with a safe conscience; which is indeed, sir, a
mender of bad soles.

MARULLUS What trade, thou knave? Thou naughty
knave, what trade?

SECOND CITIZEN Nay, I beseech you, sir, be not out
with me; yet if you be out, sir, I can mend you.

MARULLUS What meanest thou by that? Mend me,
thou saucy fellow?

SECOND CITIZEN Why, sir, cobble you.   20

FLAVIUS Thou art a cobbler, art thou?

SECOND CITIZEN Truly, sir, all that I live by is with the
awl: I meddle with no tradesman's matters, nor
women's matters; but withal I am indeed, sir, a
surgeon to old shoes; when they are in great danger,
I recover them. As proper men as ever trod upon
neat's leather have gone upon my handiwork.

[33] triumph *the ceremonial procession allowed to a Roman general to celebrate a major victory – on this occasion Caesar's victory at Munda (see p. 26).*

[35] tributaries *conquered chieftains paying tribute-money to Rome, and paraded as captives in the triumph. As Caesar had defeated fellow-Romans he had made no conquests for Rome and captured no hostile chiefs. Many Romans resented his holding a triumph for such a victory in civil war.*

[36] grace *do honour to him*
   captive bonds *the chains of captivity*

[37] senseless *incapable of feeling*

[39] Knew you not Pompey? *Have you forgotten Pompey? See p. 26.*

[40–1] Have you . . . chimney-tops *The scene is obviously Elizabethan London rather than Caesar's Rome – Dover Wilson suggests that the description was suggested by the behaviour of the London crowd celebrating the departure of Essex to subdue the Irish rebellion (see p. 2).*

[41] yea *yes, even*

[43] livelong *whole*

[44] pass *pass through*

[45] but appear *only appear – at the first glimpse*

[46] made . . . shout *shouted as one man*

[48] replication *reverberation*

[49] concave shores *hollowed-out banks – undercut by the river*

[51] cull out *pick this day. 'Cull' is generally used of picking flowers, leading to the strewing of flowers in the next line.*

[53] blood *sons (see p. 26) – with the further suggestion of their blood that has been spilt*

[56] intermit *put off, prevent*

[57] light on *fall on – as a punishment*

[58–62] Go, go . . . of all *After Marullus's threat of divine punishment, Flavius is again more conciliatory, urging them in sorrow rather than anger.*

FLAVIUS But wherefore art not in thy shop today?
Why dost thou lead these men about the
streets?

SECOND CITIZEN Truly, sir, to wear out their shoes, to   30
get myself into more work. But indeed, sir, we
make holiday to see Caesar, and to rejoice in his
triumph.

MARULLUS Wherefore rejoice? What conquest brings
he home?
What tributaries follow him to Rome,
To grace in captive bonds his chariot-wheels?
You blocks, you stones, you worse than sense-
less things!
O you hard hearts, you cruel men of Rome,
Knew you not Pompey? Many a time and oft
Have you climbed up to walls and battlements,   40
To towers and windows, yea, to chimney-
tops,
Your infants in your arms, and there have sat
The livelong day, with patient expectation,
To see great Pompey pass the streets of
Rome;
And when you saw his chariot but appear,
Have you not made an universal shout,
That Tiber trembled underneath her banks
To hear the replication of your sounds
Made in her concave shores?
And do you now put on your best attire?   50
And do you now cull out a holiday?
And do you now strew flowers in his way
That comes in triumph over Pompey's
blood?
Be gone!
Run to your houses, fall upon your knees,
Pray to the gods to intermit the plague
That needs must light on this ingratitude.

FLAVIUS Go, go, good countrymen, and for this fault

33

[59] poor . . . sort *men of your own lowly class*

[61-2] till . . . all *until the water at its lowest ebb is raised to touch the top of the highest bank*

[63] whe'r *whether*

     basest mettle *most ignoble natures – with also the suggestion of 'basest metal', 'base metals' being non-precious metals; the basest was lead, symbolic of dullness. This meaning leads on to 'guiltiness' in the next line, with a pun on 'gilt'.*

     moved *affected*

[65] Capitol *the temple of Jupiter on the Capitoline hill*

[66-7] Disrobe . . . ceremonies *strip the statues of decorations if you find them adorned with emblems celebrating Caesar's triumph. Plutarch records that 'Caesar's flatterers . . . did put diadems upon the heads of his images, supposing thereby to allure the common people to call him King, instead of Dictator'.*

[69] feast of Lupercal *the festival of purification held on 15 February in honour of the god Lupercus, protector of flocks and herds, to ensure their fertility in the coming spring. It was illegal to remove decorations put up to honour a god.*

[71] Caesar's trophies *emblems in honour of Caesar*

[72] the vulgar *the 'vulgus', the common people*

[75] an . . . pitch *to a normal height – the term used in falconry for the height to which a falcon soars before descending on its prey*

[76] above . . . men *beyond human sight, like a god*

[77] servile fearfulness *slavish dread*

ACT ONE, scene 2

The contrast with the previous scene confirms the impression already given of Caesar's dominance. He enters ceremonially, perhaps carried beneath a canopy, and probably heralded by trumpets which sound the 'sennet' and 'flourishes' – short fanfares. The mood changes from the holiday frivolity of the citizens and the expansive rhetoric of the tribunes to his short, peremptory orders (see p. 11).

for the course *stripped for running – at the Lupercalia young men ran naked through the city striking passers-by with leather thongs. It was believed that a blow from the thong could cure a woman of sterility.*

34

Assemble all the poor men of your sort;
Draw them to Tiber banks, and weep your
   tears   60
Into the channel, till the lowest stream
Do kiss the most exalted shores of all.
                     [Exeunt all the CITIZENS
See whe'r their basest mettle be not moved;
They vanish tongue-tied in their guiltiness.
Go you down that way towards the Capitol;
This way will I. Disrobe the images,
If you do find them decked with ceremonies.

MARULLUS May we do so?
     You know it is the feast of Lupercal.

FLAVIUS It is no matter; let no images   70
Be hung with Caesar's trophies. I'll about,
And drive away the vulgar from the streets;
So do you too, where you perceive them
   thick.
These growing feathers plucked from Caesar's
   wing
Will make him fly an ordinary pitch,
Who else would soar above the view of men,
And keep us all in servile fearfulness. *[Exeunt*

Scene 2. *Enter* CAESAR, ANTONY *for the course,* CAL-
PHURNIA, PORTIA, DECIUS, CICERO, BRUTUS, CASSIUS,
CASCA, *followed by a great crowd, amongst which is a*
SOÒTHSAYER; *after them* MARULLUS *and* FLAVIUS

CAESAR Calphurnia.
CASCA   Peace, ho! Caesar speaks.
CAESAR   Calphurnia.
CALPHURNIA Here, my lord.
CAESAR Stand you directly in Antonius' way
     When he doth run his course. Antonius.
ANTONY Caesar, my lord?

[6] in your speed   *because you are running so fast*

[7] elders   *men with the wisdom and authority of age*

[8] holy chase   *ritual race*

[9] sterile curse   *curse of sterility*

[11] Set on   *Proceed*

[15] press   *throng*

[16] I hear . . . music   *The Soothsayer's words have an impressively piercing quality. The warning cuts through the noisy adulation.*

[17] Caesar . . . hear   *Caesar was deaf in one ear (see l. 213), but the deliberateness with which he turns to hear increases his dignity. His practice of speaking of himself in the third person contributes perhaps to his arrogance rather than his dignity.*

[18] the ides of March   *15 March*

[19] A soothsayer . . . March   *This repetition, perhaps because of Caesar's deafness, impresses the warning on the audience. It is ironic that Brutus's first words in the play are to warn Caesar of his assassination.*

[20] Set . . . face   *implying a test – will he dare repeat it face to face with Caesar? – as well as again underlining the warning*

[24] He . . . him   *How would Caesar say this, would there be any pause? Is there any indication that he takes the warning seriously?*
Sennet   *flourish of trumpets*

[25] order . . . course   *progress of the race*

[28] gamesome   *fond of sport and frivolity. Brutus is rather contemptuous.*

[29] quick   *lively – with a suggestion of Antony's swift running, and, perhaps, of his prompt obedience to Caesar*

[30] hinder . . . desires   *keep you from your pleasures*

[32] I . . . late   *I have recently been observing you*

CAESAR Forget not, in your speed, Antonius,
    To touch Calphurnia; for our elders say
    The barren, touched in this holy chase,
    Shake off their sterile curse.

ANTONY   I shall remember.
    When Caesar says, 'Do this,' it is performed.   10

CAESAR Set on, and leave no ceremony out.

Music

SOOTHSAYER Caesar!

CAESAR Ha! Who calls?

CASCA Bid every noise be still; peace yet again!

CAESAR Who is it in the press that calls on me?
    I hear a tongue shriller than all the music
    Cry 'Caesar!' Speak; Caesar is turned to hear.

SOOTHSAYER Beware the ides of March.

CAESAR   What man is that?

BRUTUS A soothsayer bids you beware the ides of
    March.

CAESAR Set him before me; let me see his face.   20

CASSIUS Fellow, come from the throng; look upon
    Caesar.

CAESAR What say'st thou to me now? Speak once
    again.

SOOTHSAYER Beware the ides of March.

CAESAR He is a dreamer; let us leave him. Pass.

Sennet. Exeunt all except BRUTUS *and* CASSIUS

CASSIUS Will you go see the order of the course?

BRUTUS Not I.

CASSIUS I pray you, do.

BRUTUS I am not gamesome: I do lack some part
    Of that quick spirit that is in Antony.
    Let me not hinder, Cassius, your desires;   30
    I'll leave you.

CASSIUS Brutus, I do observe you now of late;
    I have not from your eyes that gentleness

[34] wont *accustomed*

[35-6] You . . . friend *Your manner has been hard (stubborn) and distant (strange). The metaphor is from horsemanship — Brutus's hand on the rein has been too hard, like that of a rider unfamiliar with his horse.*

[37-9] If . . . myself *If my looks have been clouded, my frowns have been directed only at what I see in myself*

[39] Vexed *Troubled*

[40] passions . . . difference *conflicting emotions*

[41] Conceptions . . . myself *Thoughts that concern only me. Plutarch records that there had been an estrangement between them, but for a different reason — see p. 6.*

[42] soil *blemish*

[44] Among . . . one *And you are certainly one of those friends*

[45] construe any further *seek any further explanation of*

[46] with . . . war *a prey to conflicting emotions*

[47] shows of love *outward signs of affection*

[48] mistook . . . passion *misinterpreted your feelings*

[49] By . . . whereof *Because of this misunderstanding*
     buried *concealed*

[50] worthy cogitations *reflections of great importance*

[53] by . . . things *by means of some other things — such as a mirror. Brutus takes the question literally; his interest is aroused by the sort of philosophical question that appeals to him.*

[54] 'Tis just *Just so. Cassius adopts the dispassionate tone appropriate to philosophical discussion, and turns at once to flattery.*

[56] turn *reflect*

[57] hidden *concealed only from Brutus*
     into . . . eye *into your sight*

[58] shadow *reflection*

[59] best respect *highest reputation*

[60] immortal *the first ironic suggestion that Caesar is assuming the attributes of a god — slipped in amongst the flattery to test Brutus's reaction*

[61] this . . . yoke *the oppression suffered at this time*

[62] had his eyes *could see himself as others see him, and so be aware of his virtues*

[63-5] Into what . . . in me? *Brutus is at once suspicious, perhaps because Cassius's words chime in with his own thoughts.*

And show of love as I was wont to have.
You bear too stubborn and too strange a hand
Over your friend that loves you.

BRUTUS   Cassius,
Be not deceived. If I have veiled my look,
I turn the trouble of my countenance
Merely upon myself. Vexed I am
Of late with passions of some difference,   40
Conceptions only proper to myself,
Which give some soil perhaps to my
    behaviours.
But let not therefore my good friends be
    grieved –
Among which number, Cassius, be you one –
Nor construe any further my neglect,
Than that poor Brutus, with himself at war,
Forgets the shows of love to other men.

CASSIUS Then, Brutus, I have much mistook your
    passion;
By means whereof this breast of mine hath
    buried
Thoughts of great value, worthy cogitations.   50
Tell me, good Brutus, can you see your face?

BRUTUS No, Cassius; for the eye sees not itself
But by reflection, by some other things.

CASSIUS 'Tis just;
And it is very much lamented, Brutus,
That you have no such mirrors as will turn
Your hidden worthiness into your eye,
That you might see your shadow. I have
    heard,
Where many of the best respect in Rome –
Except immortal Caesar – speaking of Brutus,   60
And groaning underneath this age's yoke,
Have wished that noble Brutus had his eyes.

BRUTUS Into what dangers would you lead me,
    Cassius,

[65] that   *the hidden worthiness*

[66] Therefore   *Cassius may be continuing from his previous speech, ignoring Brutus's interjection, or 'therefore' may imply 'since you ask that question'.*

[69] modestly discover   *reveal without exaggeration. But instead of doing so he changes the subject to that of his own worthiness.*

[71] jealous on   *suspicious of*

gentle   *noble*

[72] laughter   *source of laughter, laughing-stock. Some editions emend to 'laugher' (jester) and Dover Wilson suggests 'lover'.*

[73] stale   *make commonplace, cheapen*

ordinary   *hackneyed. As 'ordinary' was the Elizabethan term for a tavern, T. S. Dorsch suggests that this might also mean 'tavern oaths' – professions of friendship prompted by intoxication.*

[74] new protestor   *new acquaintance who protests his love*

[75] hug   *embrace*

[76] after . . . them   *afterwards slander them*

[77–8] profess . . . rout   *profess my friendship to the whole mob when warmed by banqueting*

[78] hold   *consider*

Flourish . . . shout   *The noise of the crowd acclaiming Caesar comes appropriately after Cassius's comment on those who seek popularity with 'the rout', and most opportunely for Cassius. Brutus is startled into revealing his fear of Caesar's popularity, and Cassius seizes this opportunity eagerly (l. 80).*

[85] toward . . . good   *concerning the public good*

[86–7] Set . . . indifferently   *'Indifferently' might mean 'with indifference' – he will be equally unconcerned about both death and honour, and act only for the public good – but the next two lines contradict this. It must therefore mean 'impartially', 'with equal detachment' – he will contemplate his duty to the state (which involves his honour) and the danger involved with equal calmness.*

[88] speed . . . as   *help me prosper in that*

[90] virtue   *quality, characteristic*

[91] outward favour   *external appearance*

[92] Well . . . story   *Cassius again twists Brutus's words to his own advantage, identifying honour with his personal status in Rome.*

[94] for . . . self   *speaking for myself alone*

[95] as lief . . . be   *as soon not exist. There is a contemptuous jingle of 'lief' with 'live'.*

[96] such . . . myself   *a man no different from myself*

That you would have me seek into myself
For that which is not in me?

CASSIUS Therefore, good Brutus, be prepared to hear;
And since you know you cannot see yourself
So well as by reflection, I, your glass,
Will modestly discover to yourself
That of yourself which you yet know not of.　70
And be not jealous on me, gentle Brutus:
Were I a common laughter, or did use
To stale with ordinary oaths my love
To every new protester; if you know
That I do fawn on men, and hug them ha ,
And after scandal them; or if you know
That I profess myself in banqueting
To all the rout, then hold me dangerous.

Flourish, and shout

BRUTUS What means this shouting? I do fear the
          people
      Choose Caesar for their king.

CASSIUS   Ay, do you fear it?　80
      Then must I think you would not have it so.

BRUTUS I would not, Cassius; yet I love him well.
      But wherefore do you hold me here so long?
      What is it that you would impart to me?
      If it be aught toward the general good,
      Set honour in one eye and death i' th' other,
      And I will look on both indifferently;
      For let the gods so speed me as I love
      The name of honour more than I fear death.

CASSIUS I know that virtue to be in you, Brutus,　90
      As well as I do know your outward favour.
      Well, honour is the subject of my story.
      I cannot tell what you and other men
      Think of this life; but for my single self,
      I had as lief not be as live to be
      In awe of such a thing as I myself.

[100–15] For once . . . Caesar *Caesar's skill as a swimmer is irrelevant to his fitness to rule. The fact that he was well known to be a strong swimmer further indicates that Cassius is being carried away by jealousy.*

[101] chafing with *raging against*

[105] Accoutred *Dressed*

[109] stemming . . . controversy *breasting it with hearts exulting in the contest – both with the river and with each other*

[110] arrive . . . proposed *reach the point we had agreed on*

[112–15] I . . . Caesar *Aeneas carried his father Anchises from Troy when the Greeks sacked and burnt it after the ten years' siege. According to Virgil, he subsequently sailed to Italy and founded Rome. The repetition of 'I' (ll. 112, 115) emphasises Cassius's egotism.*

[115] man *heavily emphasised*

[117] creature *subordinate – continuing the train of thought suggested by 'god': a 'creature' is a being that has been created, in contrast to 'immortal Caesar' (l. 60).*
　　　　bend his body *bow deferentially*

[119] He . . . fever *Cassius seems to have reached a conclusion, but a new recollection comes crowding in, and is interpreted with even greater malice: the pallor and shivering caused by disease is identified with that caused by cowardice. Plutarch mentions Caesar's illness in Spain – the origin of his 'falling-sickness' (see l. 255) – but describes how resolutely he resisted it.*

[120] fit *of shivering*
　　　　mark *observe*

[122] His . . . fly *In fact, of course, the colour fled from his lips, but this inversion enables Cassius to compare the lips deserting their colour to cowardly soldiers deserting their 'colours', or flag.*

[123] bend *look*

[124] his *its*

[125–6] that tongue . . . books *His eloquence moved the Romans to record his speeches – Caesar did not tell them to.*

[126] books *writing tablets*

[127] Alas *This may be part of the imitation of Caesar, or sardonic mock-sympathy.*

I was born free as Caesar, so were you;
We both have fed as well, and we can both
Endure the winter's cold as well as he:
For once, upon a raw and gusty day,   100
The troubled Tiber chafing with her shores,
Caesar said to me, 'Dar'st thou Cassius now
Leap in with me into this angry flood,
And swim to yonder point?' Upon the word,
Accoutred as I was, I plunged in,
And bade him follow; so indeed he did.
The torrent roared, and we did buffet it
With lusty sinews, throwing it aside,
And stemming it with hearts of controversy.
But ere we could arrive the point proposed,   110
Caesar cried, 'Help me, Cassius, or I sink.'
I, as Aeneas, our great ancestor,
Did from the flames of Troy upon his shoulder
The old Anchises bear, so from the waves of
    Tiber
Did I the tired Caesar. And this man
Is now become a god, and Cassius is
A wretched creature, and must bend his body
If Caesar carelessly but nod on him.
He had a fever when he was in Spain,
And when the fit was on him I did mark   120
How he did shake. 'Tis true, this god did
    shake;
His coward lips did from their colour fly,
And that same eye whose bend doth awe the
    world
Did lose his lustre; I did hear him groan;
Ay, and that tongue of his, that bade the
    Romans
Mark him and write his speeches in their
    books,
Alas, it cried, 'Give me some drink, Titinius,'
As a sick girl. Ye gods, it doth amaze me

[129] temper *temperament*

[130–1] get ... alone *leap ahead of the whole world of noble men in the race for power, and carry off the supreme prize all by himself. The shouts of the crowd again illustrate what Cassius is saying.*

[136] Colossus *a giant statue of Apollo at Rhodes, one of the seven wonders of the world. It was believed, erroneously, to have 'bestrode' the harbour entrance.*

[137] peep about *suggesting small, timorous animals*

[138] dishonourable *as they die in servitude*

[139] Men ... fates *There comes a time when man can control his fate*

[140] in ... stars *a reference to the belief that a man's character and fate are determined by the planets, especially those predominant at his birth*

[142] What should be ... ? *What special power is there ... ?*

[143] be sounded *be uttered, with the suggestion of 'resounded'*

[145] doth ... well *is as pleasant to say ('become' means 'suits')*

[146] Weigh *a pun on 'weighing one's words'*
is as heavy *has as much 'weight' or significance*
conjure *call up spirits, by using the power of names*

[147] start *raise up. Cassius implies that neither will raise a spirit; only the name of a god could do that.*

[150] Age *This age we live in*

[151] bloods *men of courageous spirit*

[152] the ... flood *Shakespeare's audience would have thought of the Flood in Genesis, but the Romans also had a legend of a flood, sent by Jove to punish human sin, which only Deucalion and his wife Pyrrha survived.*

[153] famed with *famous for*

A man of such a feeble temper should
So get the start of the majestic world, 130
And bear the palm alone.

Shout. Flourish

BRUTUS Another general shout?
I do believe that these applauses are
For some new honours that are heaped on
Caesar.
CASSIUS Why man, he doth bestride the narrow world
Like a Colossus, and we petty men
Walk under his huge legs, and peep about
To find ourselves dishonourable graves.
Men at some time are masters of their fates:
The fault, dear Brutus, is not in our stars, 140
But in ourselves, that we are underlings.
Brutus and Caesar: what should be in that
'Caesar'?
Why should that name be sounded more tnan
yours?
Write them together, yours is as fair a name;
Sound them, it doth become the mouth as
well;
Weigh them, it is as heavy; conjure with 'em,
'Brutus' will start a spirit as soon as 'Caesar'.
Now in the names of all the gods at once,
Upon what meat doth this our Caesar feed,
That he is grown so great? Age, thou art
shamed! 150
Rome, thou hast lost the breed of noble
bloods.
When went there by an age since the great
flood
But it was famed with more than with one
man?
When could they say, till now, that talked to
Rome,

[155] walks *often emended to 'walls' to match 'encompassed', but 'walks' is more appropriate to 'wide'*

[156] Now . . . enough *It may certainly be called Rome now there is so much room in it – 'Rome' was pronounced 'room'.*

[157] but . . . man *'only' repeats the sense of 'but'*

[159] a Brutus once *Lucius Junius Brutus, who took a leading part in the expulsion of the Tarquin kings from Rome, and from whom Brutus claimed descent*

       brooked *tolerated*

[160] eternal *Johnson suggested that this should be 'infernal' but the word may be used only to convey the absoluteness of his evil.*

       keep his state *maintain his court, reign*

[161] As easily *As readily*

[162] nothing jealous *not at all doubtful (see l. 71)*

[163] work *persuade*

       I have some aim *I can partly guess*

[167] moved *urged*

[170] meet *appropriate*

       high *important*

[171] chew *ruminate*

[172] villager *of no consequence, living outside Rome*

[173] repute . . . Rome *claim to be a Roman citizen*

[174–5] these . . . us *such oppression as the present circumstances are likely to inflict on us. He recognises no actual evils as yet (see II. i. 10–34).*

[176–7] struck . . . fire *excited at least this much enthusiasm. Does it sound as if Cassius is satisfied or dissatisfied with the effect of his words?*

Enter Caesar *The contrast with the earlier triumphant entry is striking.*

Train *attendants*

[180] sour *surly, bitter*

[181] proceeded . . . note *happened that is worth noting*

That her wide walks encompassed but one
man?
Now is it Rome indeed, and room enough,
When there is in it but one only man.
O, you and I have heard our fathers say,
There was a Brutus once that would have
brooked
Th' eternal devil to keep his state in Rome   160
As easily as a king.

BRUTUS That you do love me, I am nothing jealous;
What you would work me to, I have some aim;
How I have thought of this, and of these
times,
I shall recount hereafter. For this present,
I would not – so with love I might entreat
you –
Be any further moved. What you have said
I will consider; what you have to say
I will with patience hear, and find a time
Both meet to hear and answer such high
things.   170
Till then, my noble friend, chew upon this:
Brutus had rather be a villager
Than to repute himself a son of Rome
Under these hard conditions as this time
Is like to lay upon us.

CASSIUS   I am glad
That my weak words have struck but this
much show
Of fire from Brutus.

Enter CAESAR *and his Train*

BRUTUS The games are done, and Caesar is returning.
CASSIUS As they pass by, pluck Casca by the sleeve,
And he will, after his sour fashion, tell you   180
What hath proceeded worthy note today.

47

[184] chidden *scolded*

[185] Cicero *the great orator and statesman*

[186] ferret . *blood-shot and darting – like a ferret's eyes*

[188] crossed in conference *opposed in debate*

[192–5] Let me . . . dangerous *Plutarch reports Caesar as having said on one occasion, 'What will Cassius do, think ye? I like not his pale looks', and on another 'As for those fat men and smooth-combed heads, I never reckon of them. But these pale-visaged and carrion-lean people (Brutus and Cassius), I fear them most.' Consider how Caesar would speak these lines, in his present mood.*

[193] Sleek-headed *the same as 'smooth-combed' in Plutarch's account of Caesar's words*

[194] Yond *Yonder, standing over there*

[196–7] Fear . . . given *Antony's reply is typically casual, both in dismissing Cassius as a danger and in tactlessly suggesting that Caesar is capable of fear.*

[197] well given *well disposed*

[198] Would . . . fatter *Is this a serious reflection, or is Caesar passing the matter off as a joke?*

[199] my name *He again thinks of himself in the third person; he cannot fear because his name is 'Caesar'.*

liable to *susceptible to*

[201] spare *gaunt*

[202–3] looks . . . men *penetrates to their secret motives*

[204] he . . . music *The belief that a love of harmony was evidence of a harmonious character derives from Pythagoras:*

> *The man that hath no music in himself . . .*
> *Is fit for treasons, stratagems, and spoils . . .*
> *(The Merchant of Venice, V. i. 83, 5)*

Brutus, on the other hand, loves music (IV. iii. 256–9)

[205] sort *way*

[206] As . . . himself *Sardonically*

[208] at . . . ease *contented in their inmost feelings*

[213] Come . . . deaf *Plutarch says nothing of Caesar's being deaf; Shakespeare added it to contrast his arrogant boasting with his physical infirmity.*

BRUTUS I will do so. But look you, Cassius,
    The angry spot doth glow on Caesar's brow,
    And all the rest look like a chidden train:
    Calphurnia's cheek is pale, and Cicero
    Looks with such ferret and such fiery eyes
    As we have seen him in the Capitol,
    Being crossed in conference by some senators.
CASSIUS Casca will tell us what the matter is.
CAESAR Antonius.   190
ANTONY Caesar?
CAESAR Let me have men about me that are fat,
    Sleek-headed men, and such as sleep a-nights.
    Yond Cassius has a lean and hungry look;
    He thinks too much. Such men are dangerous.
ANTONY Fear him not Caesar, he's not dangerous.
    He is a noble Roman, and well given.
CAESAR Would he were fatter. But I fear him not;
    Yet if my name were liable to fear,
    I do not know the man I should avoid   200
    So soon as that spare Cassius. He reads much,
    He is a great observer, and he looks
    Quite through the deeds of men. He loves no
        plays,
    As thou dost Antony; he hears no music;
    Seldom he smiles, and smiles in such a sort
    As if he mocked himself, and scorned his
        spirit
    That could be moved to smile at any thing.
    Such men as he be never at heart's ease
    Whiles they behold a greater than themselves,
    And therefore are they very dangerous.   210
    I rather tell thee what is to be feared
    Than what I fear; for always I am Caesar.
    Come on my right hand, for this ear is deaf,
    And tell me truly what thou think'st of him.

    Sennet. Exeunt CAESAR *and his Train*

[217] chanced *happened*

[218] sad *grave*

[219] Why . . . not? *Casca's surliness produces a marked change of tone. He speaks casually in colloquial prose, pretending he cannot be bothered to describe what happened, although he seems to have observed the events closely. His repeated 'Why's' suggest contempt that anyone should bother to ask such questions.*

[220] I . . . chanced *Brutus enters into Casca's mood with quiet irony.*

[222] being offered *when it was offered*
   put it by *pushed it away*

[223] thus *He imitates the action.*
   fell a-shouting *began to shout. Plutarch says that Caesar's followers rejoiced when the crown was offered, and 'all the people together clapped their hands' when he refused it.*

[229] Ay . . . was't *Yes, certainly it was. 'Marry' was a mild oath, originally a corruption of 'by the Virgin Mary'.*

[230] gentler . . . other *more gently than the time before*
   putting-by *refusal*

[231] mine honest neighbours *Casca uses a familiar lower-class phrase contemptuously.*

[234] the manner of it *how it was done*
   gentle *noble. Brutus continues to humour Casca.*

[235] I . . . hanged as *equivalent to the modern idiom, 'I'm hanged if I can . . .'*

[236] mark *pay attention to*

[237-8] not . . . neither *The double negative was common in Elizabethan prose.*

[238] 'twas . . . coronets *According to Plutarch it was a 'laurel crown . . . having a royal band or diadem wreathed about it'.*

[239-40] to my thinking *in my opinion*

[240] fain *gladly*

[244] still *every time*
   rabblement *mob*

[245] hooted *shouted, in approval. Casca expresses his own disapproval by describing it as 'hooting'.*
   chopped *chapped, cracked by work and exposure*

[246] night-caps *soft caps, sometimes worn in the daytime*

[246-7] uttered . . . deal of *breathed out so much*

[249] swounded *swooned*

CASCA You pulled me by the cloak; would you speak
with me?

BRUTUS Ay, Casca, tell us what hath chanced today
That Caesar looks so sad.

CASCA Why, you were with him, were you not?

BRUTUS I should not then ask Casca what had chanced. 220

CASCA Why, there was a crown offered him; and,
being offered him, he put it by with the back of his
hand, thus; and then the people fell a-shouting.

BRUTUS What was the second noise for?

CASCA Why, for that too.

CASSIUS They shouted thrice; what was the last cry for?

CASCA Why, for that too.

BRUTUS Was the crown offered him thrice?

CASCA Ay, marry was't, and he put it by thrice, every
time gentler than other; and at every putting-by 230
mine honest neighbours shouted.

CASSIUS Who offered him the crown?

CASCA Why, Antony.

BRUTUS Tell us the manner of it, gentle Casca.

CASCA I can as well be hanged as tell the manner of it.
It was mere foolery; I did not mark it. I saw Mark
Antony offer him a crown; yet 'twas not a crown
neither, 'twas one of these coronets; and, as I told
you, he put it by once; but for all that, to my
thinking, he would fain have had it. Then he offered 240
it to him again; then he put it by again; but to my
thinking, he was very loath to lay his fingers off it.
And then he offered it the third time; he put it the
third time by; and still as he refused it, the rabblement hooted, and clapped their chopped hands, and
threw up their sweaty night-caps, and uttered such
a deal of stinking breath because Caesar refused
the crown, that it had almost choked Caesar; for
he swounded, and fell down at it. And for mine
own part, I durst not laugh, for fear of opening my 250
lips and receiving the bad air.

[252] soft *wait a moment. Does Cassius speak seriously or ironically?*

[255] like *likely*

falling-sickness *epilepsy (see note to l. 119)*

[257] we . . . sickness *Everyone else is falling under Caesar's domination. Cassius, as always, is quick to turn Brutus's words to his own purpose.*

[258] I . . . that *Casca is either cautious or deliberately obtuse – as part of his surly manner he refuses to recognise anything as subtle as an insinuation, but asserts the plain fact.*

[259] tag-rag *ragged – 'rag-tag' in modern English*

[261–2] as . . . theatre *For all his 'bluntness', Casca recognises Caesar's practice of dramatising himself to play on the mob's emotions.*

[266] me *the ethic dative, implying here 'in my presence', with a note of contempt*

doublet *a short jacket worn by the Elizabethans*

[266–7] offered . . . cut *a theatrical gesture showing his readiness to comply with their wishes. According to Plutarch, when he did this Caesar was 'in a rage' at the crowd's applauding his refusal of the crown. He reports a similar gesture by Caesar when annoyed by the Senate.*

[267–8] An . . . occupation *If I had been a working man*

[268] at a word *at his word – accepted his offer*

[271] done . . . amiss *while he was unconscious*

[271–2] their worships *probably expresses Casca's ironic interpretation of Caesar's deferential attitude to the crowd, rather than reporting his actual words*

[272] to think . . . infirmity *to attribute it to his unfortunate disability, and not to a deliberate intention*

[275–6] stabbed . . . mothers *There may be a bawdy allusion.*

[280] he . . . Greek *Cicero was known as 'the Grecian'.*

[282] an *if*

[283–4] those . . . heads *What does this suggest about the nature of Cicero's remarks?*

[285] it . . . me *i.e. he could not understand it. The historical Casca could speak Greek (see p. 5), but in his present surly mood Shakespeare's Casca would certainly not admit to such refinements.*

[286] scarfs *the triumphal decorations – see I. i. 66–71*

CASSIUS But soft, I pray you; what, did Caesar
    swound?

CASCA He fell down in the market-place, and foamed
  at mouth, and was speechless.

BRUTUS 'Tis very like; he hath the falling-sickness.

CASSIUS No, Caesar hath it not; but you, and I,
      And honest Casca, we have the falling-
      sickness.

CASCA I know not what you mean by that, but I am
  sure Caesar fell down. If the tag-rag people did not
  clap him and hiss him, according as he pleased 260
  and displeased them, as they use to do the players
  in the theatre, I am no true man.

BRUTUS What said he when he came unto himself?

CASCA Marry, before he fell down, when he perceived
  the common herd was glad he refused the crown, he
  plucked me ope his doublet, and offered them his
  throat to cut. An I had been a man of any occu-
  patión, if I would not have taken him at a word, I
  would I might go to hell among the rogues. And so
  he fell. When he came to himself again, he said, if 270
  he had done or said anything amiss, he desired their
  worships to think it was his infirmity. Three or four
  wenches where I stood cried, 'Alas, good soul,' and
  forgave him with all their hearts. But there's no heed
  to be taken of them; if Caesar had stabbed their
  mothers, they would have done no less.

BRUTUS And after that, he came thus sad away?

CASCA Ay.

CASSIUS Did Cicero say anything?

CASCA Ay, he spoke Greek.   280

CASSIUS To what effect?

CASCA Nay, an I tell you that, I'll ne'er look you i'
  th' face again. But those that understood him smiled
  at one another, and shook their heads; but for mine
  own part, it was Greek to me. I could tell you more
  news too: Marullus and Flavius, for pulling scarfs

[287] put to silence *perhaps executed, but Plutarch reports only that they were dismissed from office*

[291] promised forth *committed to dining out elsewhere*

[293] your mind hold *you have not changed your mind*

[298] quick mettle *a lively character*

[299] execution *the carrying out*

[301] However *However much*
     tardy form *pretence of dullness*

[302–4] This . . . appetite *This surly manner gives a piquancy to his able intelligence which makes men more ready to absorb and ruminate on what he says*

[309] think . . . world *reflect on the present state of affairs*

[311–12] Thy . . . disposed *Your noble character may be worked on and twisted from that to which it is naturally inclined (i.e. virtue). The pun on 'metal' is continued by 'wrought', used of working metal.*

[312] meet *fitting*

[313] keep . . . likes *associate only with men of similar nobility*

[314] seduced *led astray*

[315] bear me hard *bear me ill will*

[317] He *Either (a) Brutus – 'If I were loved by Caesar as Brutus is, Brutus would not be able to influence me against Caesar (as I have just been influencing Brutus)'; or (b) Caesar – 'Even if I were loved by Caesar as Brutus is, Caesar would not be able to influence me (as he influences Brutus)'. The first interpretation is supported by the fact that he goes on to plan further manipulation of Brutus; the second by a passage in Plutarch that may be the source for this speech: 'he [Brutus] might have been one of Caesar's chiefest friends . . . Howbeit, Cassius's friends did dissuade him from it . . . and prayed him to beware of Caesar's sweet enticements, and to fly his tyrannical favours; the which they said Caesar gave him, not to honour his virtue, but to weaken his constant mind, framing it to the bent of his bow' (see p. 20).*

[318] In . . . hands *In different styles of handwriting*
     several *various*

[320] tending . . . opinion *referring to the high opinion*

[321] obscurely *indirectly*

off Caesar's images, are put to silence. Fare you
well. There was more foolery yet, if I could
remember it.

CASSIUS Will you sup with me tonight, Casca?   290

CASCA No, I am promised forth.

CASSIUS Will you dine with me tomorrow?

CASCA Ay, if I be alive, and your mind hold, and your
dinner worth the eating.

CASSIUS Good; I will expect you.

CASCA Do so. Farewell both.   [Exit

BRUTUS What a blunt fellow is this grown to be!
  He was quick mettle when he went to school.

CASSIUS So is he now in execution
  Of any bold or noble enterprise,   300
  However he puts on this tardy form.
  This rudeness is a sauce to his good wit,
  Which gives men stomach to digest his words
  With better appetite.

BRUTUS And so it is. For this time I will leave you.
  Tomorrow, if you please to speak with me,
  I will come home to you; or, if you will,
  Come home to me, and I will wait for you.

CASSIUS I will do so. Till then, think of the world.
            [Exit BRUTUS
  Well, Brutus, thou art noble; yet I see   310
  Thy honourable mettle may be wrought
  From that it is disposed. Therefore 'tis meet
  That noble minds keep ever with their likes;
  For who so firm that cannot be seduced?
  Caesar doth bear me hard; but he loves Brutus.
  If I were Brutus now, and he were Cassius,
  He should not humour me. I will this night,
  In several hands, in at his windows throw,
  As if they came from several citizens,
  Writings, all tending to the great opinion   320
  That Rome holds of his name; wherein
   obscurely

[322] glanced   *hinted*
[323] seat . . . sure   *establish himself securely*
[324] worse . . . endure   *suffer worse hardships*

ACT ONE, scene 3

*The thunder and lightning follow appropriately on Cassius's
threat. Plutarch mentions all the omens of Caesar's death
described in this scene except the lion: 'fires in the element [the
sky], and spirits running up and down in the night, and also
these solitary birds to be seen at noon days sitting in the great
market-place . . . divers men were seen going up and down in
fire; and furthermore, . . . there was a slave of the soldiers,
that did cast a marvellous burning flame out of his hand, inso-
much as they that saw it thought he had been burnt, but when
the fire was out it was found he had no hurt.'*

[1] even   *evening*
     brought . . . home?   *did you accompany Caesar to his home?*
[3] sway   *realm*
[5] scolding   *raging*
[6] rived . . . oaks   *split the hard, knotted oaks*
[8] exalted with   *raised up to. As in lines 3–4, the metaphor
relates the disorder in the heavens with that in the state, caused by the
ambition of Caesar, or of the conspirators.*
[10] dropping fire   *raining down fire – lightning and other elec-
trical discharges such as St Elmo's fire*
[11] civil strife   *civil war – between either the gods or the elements
(compare ll. 7–8)*
[12] saucy with   *insolent to*
[14] Why . . . wonderful?   *Cicero is somewhat contemptuous.*
[18] sensible of   *capable of feeling*
[20] Against   *Near to*
[21] glazed   *stared, glared*
[22] annoying   *harming*
[22–3] drawn . . . heap   *drawn together into a huddled crowd*
[23] ghastly   *looking like ghosts*

Caesar's ambition shall be glanced at.
And after this, let Caesar seat him sure,
For we will shake him, or worse days endure.

[*Exit*

Scene 3. *Thunder and lightning. Enter* CASCA *and*
CICERO, *meeting*

CICERO Good even, Casca; brought you Caesar home?
Why are you breathless, and why stare you so?
CASCA Are not you moved, when all the sway of earth
Shakes like a thing unfirm? O Cicero,
I have seen tempests, when the scolding
winds
Have rived the knotty oaks, and I have seen
Th' ambitious ocean swell, and rage, and
foam,
To be exalted with the threat'ning clouds;
But never till tonight, never till now,
Did I go through a tempest dropping fire.   10
Either there is a civil strife in heaven.
Or else the world, too saucy with the gods,
Incenses them to send destruction.
CICERO Why, saw you any thing more wonderful?
CASCA A common slave – you know him well by
sight –
Held up his left hand, which did flame and
burn
Like twenty torches joined; and yet his
hand,
Not sensible of fire, remained unscorched.
Besides – I ha' not since put up my sword –
Against the Capitol I met a lion,   20
Who glazed upon me, and went surly by,
Without annoying me. And there were drawn
Upon a heap, a hundred ghastly women,

57

[24] Transformèd . . . fear *Beside themselves with fear*

[26] the bird of night *the owl*
[27] upon the market-place *above the forum*
[28] prodigies *unnatural events*
[29] conjointly *all together*
[30] These . . . natural *These are the causes of them, they are only natural events*
[31] portentous *ominous*
[32] climate *clime, region – the term used in astrology for the region controlled by a particular planet*
  that . . . upon *at which they are directed*
[33] strange-disposèd *in which strange events are prevalent*
[34] construe . . . fashion *interpret things in their own way*
[35] Clean . . . themselves *Quite differently from their real significance*

[39] sky *weather*
[40] Is not *Is not fit*

[42] what night *what a night*
[43] honest *i.e. with nothing on their consciences. As an Epicurean (see p. 19) Cassius would not believe in portents, but in this scene – perhaps for Casca's benefit – he assumes that they threaten Caesar.*

[47] Submitting me *Exposing myself. Exhilarated by the storm, Cassius again indulges in a theatrical gesture – in part to impress Casca.*
[48] unbraced *with doublet undone*

Transformèd with their fear, who swore they
   saw
Men, all in fire, walk up and down the streets.
And yesterday the bird of night did sit,
Even at noon-day, upon the market-place,
Hooting and shrieking. When these prodigies
Do so conjointly meet, let not men say,
'These are their reasons, they are natural';   30
For I believe they are portentous things
Unto the climate that they point upon.
CICERO Indeed, it is a strange-disposèd time.
   But men may construe things, after their
      fashion,
   Clean from the purpose of the things them-
      selves.
   Comes Caesar to the Capitol tomorrow?
CASCA He doth; for he did bid Antonius
   Send word to you he would be there to-
      morrow.
CICERO Good night then, Casca; this disturbèd sky
   Is not to walk in.
CASCA   Farewell Cicero.   40
                    [*Exit* CICERO

Enter CASSIUS

CASSIUS Who's there?
CASCA   A Roman.
CASSIUS   Casca, by your voice.
CASCA Your ear is good. Cassius, what night is this!
CASSIUS A very pleasing night to honest men.
CASCA Who ever knew the heavens menace so?
CASSIUS Those that have known the earth so full of
   faults.
   For my part, I have walked about the streets,
   Submitting me unto the perilous night;
   And, thus unbraced, Casca, as you see,

[49] thunder-stone   *thunderbolt*

[50] cross   *forked*

[52] Even in the aim   *Right in its path*

[53] tempt   *provoke, challenge*

[54] part   *role, duty*

[55] tokens   *symbols*

[56] heralds   *portents – heralding what is to come*
astonish   *stun, dismay*

[57] dull   *stupid. Having demonstrated his own intrepidity he sets out to provoke Casca to emulate him.*

[58] want   *lack*

[59] you use not   *you do not exercise them*
gaze   *stare*

[60] put on   *show*
in wonder   *into a state of amazement*

[61] impatience   *restlessness*

[64] from . . . kind   *depart from the natural characteristics and behaviour of their species. In his excitement Cassius is speaking in a rapid, disjointed manner. Verbs have to be supplied for several of these clauses.*

[65] old . . . children   *The meaning may be that the portents are so obvious that even dotards, fools and infants can interpret them, but all three were attributed with the power of prophecy – natural idiots, in particular, were believed to have special powers of insight.*
calculate   *prognosticate – originally by astrological calculations*

[66] their ordinance   *natural behaviour ordained for them*

[67] pre-formed faculties   *innate characteristics*

[68] To monstrous quality   *Into unnatural modes of behaviour*

[69] infused . . . spirits   *imbued them with these characteristics*

[71] Unto . . . state   *About some unnatural state of affairs*

[75] lion . . . Capitol   *perhaps the lion seen by Casca (l. 20), or an allusion to the celebrated lions that were kept in the Tower of London, which Shakespeare may have associated with the Capitol as it was thought erroneously to have been founded by Julius Caesar.*

[77] personal action   *his own deeds*
prodigious   *ominous, threatening*

[78] strange eruptions   *unnatural outbreaks*

Have bared my bosom to the thunder-stone;
And when the cross blue lightning seemed to
  open   50
The breast of heaven, I did present myself
Even in the aim and very flash of it.

CASCA But wherefore did you so much tempt the
  heavens?
It is the part of men to fear and tremble
When the most mighty gods by tokens send
Such dreadful heralds to astonish us.

CASSIUS You are dull, Casca, and those sparks of life
That should be in a Roman you do want,
Or else you use not. You look pale, and gaze,
And put on fear, and cast yourself in wonder, 60
To see the strange impatience of the heavens;
But if you would consider the true cause
Why all these fires, why all these gliding
  ghosts,
Why birds and beasts from quality and kind,
Why old men, fools, and children calculate,
Why all these things change from their
  ordinance,
Their natures, and pre-formèd faculties,
To monstrous quality – why, you shall find
That heaven hath infused them with these
  spirits
To make them instruments of fear and
  warning   70
Unto some monstrous state.
Now could I, Casca, name to thee a man
Most like this dreadful night,
That thunders, lightens, opens graves, and
  roars
As doth the lion in the Capitol;
A man no mightier than thyself, or me,
In personal action, yet prodigious grown,
And fearful, as these strange eruptions are.

JULIUS CAESAR

[79] 'Tis Caesar . . . Cassius? *Casca sounds subdued, nervously seeking reassurance.*

[81] thews *sinews*

[82] woe the while *alas for these times*

[84] Our . . . sufferance *Our oppression and the way we suffer it*

[87–8] And . . . Italy *from Plutarch (see note to II. ii. 93–101)*

[89] wear . . . dagger *sheathed in his own body*

[90–100] Cassius . . . pleasure *How far is this a genuine response, and how far is it put on to impress Casca? In his more theatrical moods Cassius, like Caesar, speaks of himself in the third person.*

[91] Therein *In this respect, by this means*

[95] be . . . spirit *hold back a resolute spirit*

[96] worldly bars *restrictions of this life*

[97] dismiss *free – bid farewell to these restrictions*

[98] know . . . besides *let all the world know – another grandly rhetorical statement, which is echoed by the thunder at the end of the speech*

[99] That . . . bear *The tyranny as it affects me*

[101] bondman *prisoner – in bonds*

[102] cancel *a legal term for the annulment of a bond (picking up this sense in 'bondman'), in this case the bond that holds him in servitude*

[104] Poor man *ironic sympathy, as if Caesar were forced to be a tyrant by the weakness of the Romans*

[106] were no *would not be*

     hinds *both female deer and servants*

[108] trash *twigs – waste from timber*

CASCA 'Tis Caesar that you mean, is it not, Cassius?

CASSIUS Let it be who it is: for Romans now   80
    Have thews and limbs like to their ancestors,
    But, woe the while, our fathers' minds are
      dead,
    And we are governed with our mothers'
      spirits;
    Our yoke and sufferance show us womanish.

CASCA Indeed, they say the senators tomorrow
    Mean to establish Caesar as a king;
    And he shall wear his crown by sea and land,
    In every place, save here in Italy.

CASSIUS I know where I will wear this dagger then;
    Cassius from bondage will deliver Cassius.   90
    Therein, ye gods, you make the weak most
      strong;
    Therein, ye gods, you tyrants do defeat.
    Nor stony tower, nor walls of beaten brass,
    Nor airless dungeon, nor strong links of iron,
    Can be retentive to the strength of spirit;
    But life, being weary of these worldly bars,
    Never lacks power to dismiss itself.
    If I know this, know all the world besides,
    That part of tyranny that I do bear
    I can shake off at pleasure.

Thunder

CASCA   So can I;   100
    So every bondman in his own hand bears
    The power to cancel his captivity.

CASSIUS And why should Caesar be a tyrant then?
    Poor man, I know he would not be a wolf,
    But that he sees the Romans are but sheep;
    He were no lion, were not Romans hinds.
    Those that with haste will make a mighty
      fire
    Begin it with weak straws. What trash is Rome,

[109] offal   *chips of wood*

[110] base matter   *the material from which the fire starts, on which it is 'based' – also implying 'degraded'*

   illuminate   *contribute to the glory of*

[111–12] O grief . . . me?   *His grief has induced him to speak indiscreetly.*

[113] willing bondman   *a man willing to be a slave, who might therefore betray Cassius to Caesar. The fear is of course feigned, it is Cassius's last gesture to sting Casca into declaring himself.*

[114] My . . . made   *I shall have to answer for my rash words*

   armed   *in virtuous resolution*

[115] indifferent   *of no concern*

[117] fleering   *sneering, disloyal*

   my hand   *He offers his hand as a pledge.*

[118] Be . . . griefs   *Gather a party to remedy all these grievances*

[119–20] set . . . farthest   *be as deeply involved as any man*

[121] moved   *persuaded, incited*

[123] undergo   *undertake*

[124] honourable . . . consequence   *the effect of which will be both honourable and dangerous*

[125] by this . . . stay   *by this time they wait*

[126] Pompey's porch   *porch of the theatre built by Pompey in the Campus Martius, outside the gates of Rome*

[128] complexion . . . element   *character of the sky – for 'complexion', see note to V. v. 73–4*

[129] In favour's   *In appearance is*

[131] Stand close   *Stay out of sight*

[132] gait   *walk*

[134] find out   *look for*

[135–6] incorporate . . . attempts   *united with us in our enterprise*

[136] stayed   *waited*

[137–8] I am glad . . . sights   *In his haste, and distracted by the storm, Cinna ignores Cassius's question.*

What rubbish, and what offal, when it serves
For the base matter to illuminate   110
So vile a thing as Caesar! But, O grief,
Where hast thou led me? I, perhaps, speak this
Before a willing bondman; then I know
My answer must be made. But I am armed,
And dangers are to me indifferent.

CASCA You speak to Casca, and to such a man
That is no fleering tell-tale. Hold, my hand;
Be factious for redress of all these griefs,
And I will set this foot of mine as far
As who goes farthest.

CASSIUS   There's a bargain made. 120
Now know you, Casca, I have moved already
Some certain of the noblest-minded Romans
To undergo with me an enterprise
Of honourable-dangerous consequence;
And I do know by this, they stay for me
In Pompey's porch; for now, this fearful night,
There is no stir or walking in the streets;
And the complexion of the element
In favour's like the work we have in hand,
Most bloody, fiery, and most terrible. 130

Enter CINNA

CASCA Stand close awhile, for here comes one in haste.

CASSIUS 'Tis Cinna; I do know him by his gait.
He is a friend. Cinna, where haste you so?

CINNA To find out you. Who's that? Metellus Cimber?

CASSIUS No, it is Casca, one incorporate
To our attempts. Am I not stayed for, Cinna?

CINNA I am glad on't. What a fearful night is this!

[142] Be . . . content *Set your mind at rest about that*

[142–8] Be you . . . Trebonius there? *From Plutarch: 'his friends . . . by many bills also, did openly call and procure him to do that he did. For under the image of his ancestor Junius Brutus . . . they wrote, "O, that it pleased the gods thou wert now alive, Brutus", and again, "that thou wert here among us now" . . . His tribunal or chair, where he gave audience during the time he was Praetor, was full of such bills – "Brutus, thou art asleep, and art not Brutus indeed."'*

[143] praetor's chair *the official seat of the praetor, an office held by Brutus. A praetor was a magistrate.*

[144] Where . . . it *Where only Brutus may find it*

[145] Set . . . wax *Fasten it with wax*

[146] old Brutus' statue *the statue of Junius Brutus (see note to I. ii. 159)*

[147] Repair *Make your way*

[150] hie *hasten*

[151] bestow *distribute*

[155–6] the man . . . ours *he will be won over completely at the next meeting*

[157] sits high *is highly esteemed*

[158] offence *a crime*

[159] countenance *both 'face' and 'approval'*

alchemy *the medieval science concerned with the transmutation of base metals into gold*

[162] conceited *understood (conceived) and aptly expressed. A 'conceit' was an ingenious metaphor.*

[164] of him *of his support*

There's two or three of us have seen strange
    sights.
CASSIUS Am I not stayed for? Tell me.
CINNA   Yes, you are.
    O Cassius, if you could   140
    But win the noble Brutus to our party –
CASSIUS Be you content. Good Cinna, take this
    paper,
    And look you lay it in the praetor's chair,
    Where Brutus may but find it. And throw
    this
    In at his window. Set this up with wax
    Upon old Brutus' statue. All this done,
    Repair to Pompey's porch, where you shall
    find us.
    Is Decius Brutus and Trebonius there?
CINNA All but Metullus Cimber, and he's gone
    To seek you at your house. Well, I will hie,   150
    And so bestow these papers as you bade
    me.
CASSIUS That done, repair to Pompey's theatre.
                         [*Exit* CINNA
    Come Casca, you and I will yet ere day
    See Brutus at his house. Three parts of him
    Is ours already, and the man entire
    Upon the next encounter yields him ours.
CASCA O, he sits high in all the people's hearts;
    And that which would appear offence in
    us,
    His countenance, like richest alchemy,
    Will change to virtue and to worthiness.   160
CASSIUS Him and his worth, and our great need of
    him
    You have right well conceited. Let us go,
    For it is after midnight; and ere day
    We will awake him, and be sure of him.
                            [*Exeunt*

ACT TWO, scene 1

*The storm, that in the previous scene corresponded to the dis-
order in the state, has abated, but the heavens are still disturbed
(l. 44) and the stars hidden (ll. 2–3), symbolising the conflict
and darkness in Brutus's mind. External tumult – and Cassius's
expansive rhetorical gestures – have been replaced by a deeper
psychological disorder. For the symbolism of light and sleep
associated with Lucius, see p. 25.*

orchard   *garden*

[2] progress . . . stars   *movement across the sky*

[5] When   *an impatient exclamation – 'When are you coming?'*

[7] taper   *candle.*

     study   *The study suggests the peaceful scholarship from which
Brutus has been drawn to grapple with public affairs.*

[10] It . . . death   *Only Caesar's death can ensure the freedom of
Rome. He seems convinced already (see I. iii. 154–5).*

[11] spurn at   *strike at, attack – literally, kick*

[12] general   *general good of the state*
     would be   *wishes to be*

[13] there's the question   *that is the point*

[14] the bright . . . adder   *sunshine (good fortune, popularity)
hatches the snake (danger of tyranny)*

[15] craves   *calls for*
     that   *either 'that's the crucial issue', or, as Dover Wilson
suggests, an exclamation of disgust. The First Folio has 'Crown him
that' which could mean 'Crown him king', Brutus being unwilling
even to say the word.*

[16] put . . . him   *give him the power to harm us*

[17] at his will   *whenever he wishes*

[18–19] Th' abuse . . . power   *Authority is misused when its
power is exercised without compassion*

[20–1] affections . . . reason   *when his passions and desires controlled him more than his reason*

[21] a common proof   *common experience*

[22] lowliness . . . ladder   *it is by behaving with humility that
the ambitious first climb to power*

[23] turns his face   *pays special attention*

[24] upmost round   *topmost rung*

ACT TWO

Scene I. *Enter* BRUTUS *in his orchard*

BRUTUS What, Lucius, ho!
    I cannot, by the progress of the stars,
    Give guess how near to day. Lucius, I say!
    I would it were my fault to sleep so soundly.
    When, Lucius, when? Awake, I say! What,
      Lucius!

Enter LUCIUS

LUCIUS Called you, my lord?
BRUTUS Get me a taper in my study, Lucius;
    When it is lighted, come and call me here.
LUCIUS I will, my lord.

                                [*Exit*

BRUTUS It must be by his death; and for my part,   10
    I know no personal cause to spurn at him,
    But for the general. He would be crowned:
    How that might change his nature, there's the
      question.
    It is the bright day that brings forth the adder,
    And that craves wary walking. Crown him?
      – that;
    And then, I grant, we put a sting in him,
    That at his will he may do danger with.
    Th' abuse of greatness is when it disjoins
    Remorse from power; and, to speak truth of
      Caesar,
    I have not known when his affections swayed   20
    More than his reason. But 'tis a common
      proof
    That lowliness is young ambition's ladder,
    Whereto the climber-upward turns his face;
    But when he once attains the upmost round,

[26] base degrees   *lower steps (offices) through which he rose*

[28] prevent   *anticipate, and so forestall*
[28-9] the quarrel . . . is   *the complaint against Caesar cannot be justified by his present behaviour*
[30] Fashion it thus   *Put it this way*
[30-1] what . . . extremities   *if his present power were increased it would lead him into such and such tyrannical excesses*

[33] as his kind   *according to its nature*
      mischievous   *harmful*

[35] taper   *candle*
      closet   *study*
[36] window   *window-sill*
      flint   *The candle would be lit with a flint and tinder.*
[37] This paper   *See I. iii. 144-5.*

[40] the ides of March   *recalling the Soothsayer's prophecy*

[44] exhalations   *perhaps meteors, as well as the 'fires' referred to in I. iii. (10, 63), all of which were thought to be 'exhaled', or drawn out by the sun, from the earth. The light is eerie and disturbing – meteors were portents of disaster.*
      whizzing   *hissing*
[46] Brutus . . . sleep'st   *See note to I. iii. 142-8.*
      see thyself   *Compare I. ii. 55-62*
[47] &c   *He skims through the letters, omitting parts of them – he has read this sort of thing before (ll. 49-50).*
      redress   *correct what is wrong*
[49] instigations   *incitements to action*
[51] piece it out   *fill in the gaps. The letters express their theme indirectly (see I. ii. 321-2).*

He then unto the ladder turns his back,
Looks in the clouds, scorning the base degrees
By which he did ascend. So Caesar may;
Then lest he may, prevent. And since the
    quarrel
Will bear no colour for the thing he is,
Fashion it thus: that what he is, augmented,   30
Would run to these and these extremities;
And therefore think him as a serpent's egg,
Which, hatched, would, as his kind, grow
    mischievous,
And kill him in the shell.

Enter LUCIUS

LUCIUS The taper burneth in your closet, sir.
Searching the window for a flint, I found
This paper, thus sealed up; and I am sure
It did not lie there when I went to bed.

Gives him the letter

BRUTUS Get you to bed again; it is not day.
Is not tomorrow, boy, the ides of March?   40
LUCIUS I know not, sir.
BRUTUS Look in the calendar, and bring me word.
LUCIUS I will, sir.

[Exit

BRUTUS The exhalations whizzing in the air
Give so much light that I may read by them.

Opens the letter and reads

'Brutus, thou sleep'st; awake, and see thyself.
Shall Rome, &c. Speak, strike, redress.'
'Brutus, thou sleep'st; awake!'
Such instigations have been often dropped
Where I have took them up.   50
'Shall Rome &c.' Thus must I piece it out:

[52] under . . . awe   *in awe of one man*

[53-4] My . . . king   *See note to I. ii. 159.*

[57-8] If . . . Brutus   *If my actions will produce the desired reform, then you will receive the whole of your request (i.e. he will certainly 'speak' and 'strike', but the third part of the request depends on the success of his action). This is a solemn vow, but it is ironic that it should be the fabricated letters that should have finally convinced him.*

[59] wasted . . . days   *fifteen days have passed. Lucius includes the day that is about to break.*
  within   *off stage*

[61] whet   *incite. To 'whet' a knife is to sharpen it.*
[64] motion   *impulse or prompting to act*
  interim   *interval*
[65] phantasma   *nightmare*
[66] genius   *the guardian spirit allotted to a man at birth to guide his actions – a concept familiar to both the Romans and the Elizabethans (Shakespeare also refers to it in Macbeth, III. i. 55, and Antony and Cleopatra, II. iii. 18-29). As this speech describes the conflict within a man, it might be equated with the soul.*
  mortal instruments   *bodily faculties – 'mortal' in contrast to the immortal spirit or soul*
[67] council   *debate – obviously a violent one here, the 'mortal instruments' (emotions as well as senses and physical powers) are like counsellors rebelling against the sovereign spirit. It is not clear which side is in the right.*
  state   *realm – not merely condition. The image of an 'insurrection' relates psychological disorder to political disorder, as both have previously been related to the cosmic disorder in the heavens. See I. iii. 3-8.*
[70] brother   *brother-in-law. Cassius had married Junia, Brutus's sister.*
[72] moe   *more*

Shall Rome stand under one man's awe?
  What, Rome?
My ancestors did from the streets of Rome
The Tarquin drive, when he was called a
  king.
'Speak, strike, redress.' Am I entreated
To speak, and strike? O Rome, I make thee
  promise,
If the redress will follow, thou receivest
Thy full petition at the hand of Brutus.

Enter LUCIUS

LUCIUS Sir, March is wasted fifteen days.

Knocking within

BRUTUS 'Tis good. Go to the gate; somebody knocks.   60
                    [*Exit* LUCIUS
Since Cassius first did whet me against
  Caesar,
I have not slept.
Between the acting of a dreadful thing
And the first motion, all the interim is
Like a phantasma, or a hideous dream.
The genius and the mortal instruments
Are then in council; and the state of man,
Like to a little kingdom, suffers then
The nature of an insurrection.

Enter LUCIUS

LUCIUS Sir, 'tis your brother Cassius at the door,   70
  Who doth desire to see you.
BRUTUS   Is he alone?
LUCIUS No, sir, there are moe with him.
BRUTUS   Do you know them?

[73] hats *This is often thought an anachronism, but the Romans did wear headgear that might be called 'hats'.*

[75] discover *distinguish, identify*
[76] mark of favour *distinctive feature of their appearance*

[77] the faction *the conspiratorial party – see I. iii. 118*

[79] evils . . . free *evil beings can move freely abroad*

[81] mask . . . visage *conceal your unnatural face. Brutus still regards conspiracy as 'unnatural' even though he has been persuaded to support this one.*

[83] path *walk, follow your course – often emended to 'put', but there are other examples of this use of 'path'*
    thy . . . on *wearing your natural appearance*
[84] Erebus *the dark region between earth and Hades, the underworld of classical mythology*
[85] prevention *being forestalled and thwarted*

[86] bold . . . rest *too presumptuous in disturbing your sleep*

[91–3] every . . . you *Compare I. ii. 55–62.*

[94–6] This is . . . Cimber *Brutus knows his visitors, but their disguise provides a pretext for introducing them to the audience.*

LUCIUS No, sir, their hats are plucked about their
    ears,
    And half their faces buried in their cloaks,
    That by no means I may discover them
    By any mark of favour.
BRUTUS   Let 'em enter.

             [Exit LUCIUS

    They are the faction. O conspiracy,
    Sham'st thou to show thy dangerous brow by
     night,
    When evils are most free? O, then by day
    Where wilt thou find a cavern dark enough 80
    To mask thy monstrous visage? Seek none,
     conspiracy;
    Hide it in smiles and affability;
    For if thou path, thy native semblance on,
    Not Erebus itself were dim enough
    To hide thee from prevention.

Enter the conspirators, CASSIUS, CASCA, DECIUS, CINNA,
METELLUS CIMBER, *and* TREBONIUS

CASSIUS I think we are too bold upon your rest.
    Good morrow, Brutus; do we trouble you?
BRUTUS I have been up this hour, awake all night.
    Know I these men that come along with you?
CASSIUS Yes, every man of them; and no man here 90
    But honours you; and every one doth wish
    You had but that opinion of yourself
    Which every noble Roman bears of you.
    This is Trebonius.
BRUTUS   He is welcome hither.
CASSIUS This, Decius Brutus.
BRUTUS   He is welcome too.
CASSIUS This, Casca; this, Cinna; and this, Metellus
    Cimber.
BRUTUS They are all welcome.

[98] watchful cares *worries that keep you awake*

[98–9] interpose . . . night *hinder your eyes from closing*

[100] Shall . . . word? *May I request a word in private? Cassius still has to ensure that Brutus is wholly theirs (see I. iii. 154–6).*

[101–11] Here lies . . . directly here *This discussion covers the conversation of Brutus and Cassius, but, as they need not have whispered, its real dramatic purpose is to convey the tension amongst the conspirators and to paint the scene, with the first streaks of dawn symbolising their hopes now that Brutus has joined them. In identifying the 'high east' (l. 110), suggesting 'high hopes', Casca points significantly with his sword at the Capitol, where Caesar will be murdered. In some productions he indicates Brutus at l. 106, making the episode more explicitly symbolic.*

[102] No *– the blunt Casca*

[104] fret *interlace, adorn*

[105] confess . . . deceived *admit that you are both mistaken*

[107] a great . . . on *a considerable distance toward*

[108] Weighing . . . year *Considering that it is spring*

[110] first . . . fire *rises*

high east *due east*

[112] all over *all of you*

[114] No . . . oath *Brutus speaks peremptorily – this is the first of three occasions when he overrules Cassius.*

[114–16] If . . . weak *If the suffering evident in men's faces, the suffering we feel ourselves, and the corruption of this age are inadequate motives*

[116] betimes *at once*

[117] idle bed *bed of idleness*

[118] high-sighted *looking from a great height, as a falcon seeks its prey – suggesting both pride and power*

range *roam, seeking its prey*

[119] by lottery *by chance – at the tyrant's whim*

[121] kindle *incite. 'Bear fire', 'kindle' and 'steel' all suggest the kindling of fire with flint and steel.*

[124] prick . . . redress *urge us to put right what is wrong*

[125] secret *discreet, able to keep secrets*

spoke the word *given our words*

[126] palter *equivocate, deceive*

[127] honesty . . . engaged *the word of one honest man to another*

[128] this . . . it *we shall realise our aim or die in the attempt*

What watchful cares do interpose themselves
Betwixt your eyes and night?

CASSIUS Shall I entreat a word?　　　　　　　　　1

BRUTUS and CASSIUS whisper

DECIUS Here lies the east; doth not the day break
　　　here?

CASCA No.

CINNA O pardon sir, it doth; and yon grey lines
　　　That fret the clouds are messengers of day.

CASCA You shall confess that you are both deceived.
　　　Here, as I point my sword, the sun arises,
　　　Which is a great way growing on the south,
　　　Weighing the youthful season of the year.
　　　Some two months hence, up higher toward
　　　　the north
　　　He first presents his fire; and the high east　　110
　　　Stands, as the Capitol, directly here.

BRUTUS Give me your hands all over, one by one.

CASSIUS And let us swear our resolution.

BRUTUS No, not an oath. If not the face of men,
　　　The sufferance of our souls, the time's abuse –
　　　If these be motives weak, break off betimes,
　　　And every man hence to his idle bed.
　　　So let high-sighted tyranny range on,
　　　Till each man drop by lottery. But if these,
　　　As I am sure they do, bear fire enough　　　120
　　　To kindle cowards, and to steel with valour
　　　The melting spirits of women, then, country-
　　　　men,
　　　What need we any spur but our own cause,
　　　To prick us to redress? What other bond
　　　Than secret Romans, that have spoke the
　　　　word,
　　　And will not palter? And what other oath
　　　Than honesty to honesty engaged,
　　　That this shall be, or we will fall for it?

77

[129] Swear priests *Make priests swear*
       cautelous *crafty*

[130] carrions *so decrepit that they are nearly corpses*

[130–1] such . . . wrongs *men who are so submissive that they seem to welcome injuries*

[131–2] unto . . . doubt *make wretches whose honesty is already doubted take oaths in enterprises that are evil (and therefore less likely to inspire loyalty). Brutus takes his examples to an extreme. His whole protest is unnecessarily extravagant, when he should be concerned with immediate practical matters.*

[132] stain *mar*

[133] even *uniform – virtuous all through*

[134] insuppressive mettle *insuppressible determination*

[135] or . . . performance *either our cause or the way we carry it out*

[138] guilty . . . bastardy *each drop is individually guilty of not being true Roman blood*

[140] hath . . . him *he has given*

[141–2] But what . . . with us *Cassius does not answer Brutus.*

[142] stand . . . us *support us strongly*

[144–6] his . . . deeds *his age and distinction will gain us a good reputation and persuade men to approve our actions. The extended metaphor ('silver', 'purchase', 'buy') suggests that the silver of his hair will bribe men to respect them.*

[147] ruled our hands *directed our actions*

[148] youths *youth*
       no . . . appear *not be noticed at all*

[149] buried . . . gravity *concealed beneath his seriousness. There is a pun on 'grave' in 'gravity'.*

[150] break with *broach the matter to him*

[150–2] O name . . . begin *For the irony here see p. 16. Plutarch says that Cicero was excluded because of his cowardice.*

[152] Then leave him out *Cassius changes his opinion very rapidly, perhaps to humour Brutus. Casca again echoes him (see l. 143).*

[155] well urged *a good suggestion*

[157] of *in*

[158] shrewd contriver *cunning plotter*
       means *resources*

[159] improve them *makes the most of them*

[160] annoy *harm*

Swear priests and cowards, and men cautelous,
Old feeble carrions, and such suffering souls   130
That welcome wrongs; unto bad causes swear
Such creatures as men doubt; but do not stain
The even virtue of our enterprise,
Nor th' insuppressive mettle of our spirits,
To think that or our cause or our performance
Did need an oath; when every drop of blood
That every Roman bears, and nobly bears,
Is guilty of a several bastardy
If he do break the smallest particle
Of any promise that hath passed from him.   140

CASSIUS But what of Cicero? Shall we sound him?
I think he will stand very strong with us.

CASCA Let us not leave him out.

CINNA   No, by no means.

METELLUS O, let us have him, for his silver hairs
Will purchase us a good opinion,
And buy men's voices to commend our deeds.
It shall be said his judgement ruled our
  hands;
Our youths and wildness shall no whit
  appear,
But all be buried in his gravity.

BRUTUS O name him not; let us not break with him; 150
For he will never follow any thing
That other men begin.

CASSIUS   Then leave him out.

CASCA Indeed he is not fit.

DECIUS Shall no man else be touched but only
  Caesar?

CASSIUS Decius, well urged. I think it is not meet
Mark Antony, so well beloved of Caesar,
Should outlive Caesar. We shall find of him
A shrewd contriver; and you know, his means,
If he improve them, may well stretch so far
As to annoy us all; which to prevent,   160

[162–89] Our course ... company *Plutarch quotes this as Brutus's first mistake, but gives as his reasons that 'it was not honest' and that Antony 'being a noble-minded and courageous man ... would willingly help his country to recover her liberty'.*

[162] course *course of action*

[164] Like ... afterwards *as if they were killing Caesar in anger and then venting their malice on his friends*

[166] Let ... sacrificers *They are killing Caesar for a sacred cause, as a priest sacrifices his victim. Brutus's idealism blinds him to practical dangers.*

Caius *He addresses Cassius affectionately, if perhaps a little patronisingly, by his first name – perhaps because this is the third time he has overruled him.*

[167] the spirit of Caesar *what Caesar stands for – tyranny*

[169] come by *gain possession of*

[171] gentle *noble*

[173–4] Let's carve ... hounds *In hunting, deer were carved ceremoniously – as a sacrificial animal was carved for the gods – while quarry of less dignity were hewn up for the hounds.*

[175–7] And let ... chide 'em *Their hearts must incite their limbs (their 'servants' – the 'mortal instruments' of l. 66) to commit the murder, but afterwards show their regret by appearing to reprove their limbs for having done so. It is ironic that Brutus's metaphor suggests that this regret will be hypocritical.*

[177–8] make ... envious *make it clear that we acted out of necessity, and not hatred*

[180] purgers *surgeons who are curing Rome of her political disease by letting blood*

[181] And for ... him *The tone is casually contemptuous.*

[183–4] Yet I ... Caesar *Cassius readily accepts his first two rebuffs but he feels that this is more important.*

[184] ingrafted *deeply rooted – continuing the metaphor of Antony as a limb, or branch, of Caesar*

[185] Alas ... Cassius *The tone is even more patronising.*

[187] to himself *against himself*

take thought *grieve, take it to heart*

[188] that ... should *that would be much to expect from him*

[190] no fear in *nothing to fear from*

Let Antony and Caesar fall together.

BRUTUS Our course will seem too bloody, Caius
      Cassius,
To cut the head off and then hack the limbs,
Like wrath in death and envy afterwards;
For Antony is but a limb of Caesar.
Let us be sacrificers, but not butchers, Caius.
We all stand up against the spirit of Caesar,
And in the spirit of men there is no blood;
O, that we then could come by Caesar's spirit,
And not dismember Caesar! But, alas,   170
Caesar must bleed for it. And, gentle friends,
Let's kill him boldly, but not wrathfully;
Let's carve him as a dish fit for the gods,
Not hew him as a carcass fit for hounds.
And let our hearts, as subtle masters do,
Stir up their servants to an act of rage,
And after seem to chide 'em. This shall make
Our purpose necessary, and not envious;
Which so appearing to the common eyes,
We shall be called purgers, not murderers.   180
And for Mark Antony, think not of him;
For he can do no more than Caesar's arm
When Caesar's head is off.

CASSIUS   Yet I fear him;
For in the ingrafted love he bears to Caesar –

BRUTUS Alas, good Cassius, do not think of him.
If he love Caesar, all that he can do
Is to himself, take thought, and die for
      Caesar.
And that were much he should; for he is
      given
To sports, to wildness, and much company.

TREBONIUS There is no fear in him; let him not die,   190
For he will live, and laugh at this hereafter.

Clock strikes

JULIUS CAESAR

[195] he . . . late *Compare I. ii. 1–9. There is no warrant for this in Plutarch.*

[196] Quite from *In direct opposition to*

main *strong*

[197] fantasy *fanciful illusions*

ceremonies *predictions of the future by means of religious rituals*

[198] apparent prodigies *wonders that have appeared*

[200] augurers *augurs – priests who interpreted omens*

[201] hold *keep*

[203] o'ersway him *change his mind*

[204] unicorns . . . trees *According to medieval fables, the hunter stood in front of a tree and then dodged aside so that the unicorn ran its horn into the trunk.*

[205] bears with glasses *Bears could be captured after they had been bewildered by being shown their reflections in mirrors.*

holes *concealed pits into which the elephant falls*

[206] toils *snares*

men . . . with flatterers *i.e. just as the strongest animals have specific weaknesses by which they may be trapped, so men may be betrayed by flattery.*

[209] work *work on him. Decius pauses to savour his cunning.*

[210] give . . . humour *shape his mood in the right way*

[213] uttermost *latest time*

[215] bear . . . hard *hates Caesar. Plutarch reports that Caius Ligarius, a friend of Brutus, had been acquitted by Caesar for supporting Pompey, but still resented the tyrannical power that had put him in danger.*

[216] rated *strongly reproved*

[218] by him *by way of his house*

[219] reasons *for loving Brutus*

[220] Send . . . hither *Only send him here*

fashion him *shape him to our purposes*

82

BRUTUS Peace, count the clock.
CASSIUS   The clock hath stricken three.
TREBONIUS 'Tis time to part.
CASSIUS   But it is doubtful yet,
        Whether Caesar will come forth today or no;
        For he is superstitious grown of late,
        Quite from the main opinion he held once
        Of fantasy, of dreams, and ceremonies.
        It may be these apparent prodigies,
        The unaccustomed terror of this night,
        And the persuasion of his augurers,   200
        May hold him from the Capitol today.
DECIUS Never fear that; if he be so resolved,
        I can o'ersway him; for he loves to hear
        That unicorns may be betrayed with trees,
        And bears with glasses, elephants with holes,
        Lions with toils, and men with flatterers;
        But when I tell him he hates flatterers,
        He says he does, being then most flattered.
        Let me work;
        For I can give his humour the true bent,   210
        And I will bring him to the Capitol.
CASSIUS Nay, we will all of us be there to fetch him.
BRUTUS By the eighth hour; is that the uttermost?
CINNA Be that the uttermost, and fail not then.
METELLUS Caius Ligarius doth bear Caesar hard,
        Who rated him for speaking well of Pompey;
        I wonder none of you have thought of him.
BRUTUS Now, good Metellus, go along by him.
        He loves me well, and I have given him reasons;
        Send him but hither, and I'll fashion him.   220
CASSIUS The morning comes upon's. We'll leave you,
        Brutus.
        And, friends, disperse yourselves; but all
        remember
        What you have said, and show yourselves true
        Romans.

[225] put . . . purposes *reflect our intentions*

[226] bear it *carry it off*

[227] untired spirits *unflagging resolution*
formal constancy *a consistent appearance of composure*

[230] honey-heavy dew *sweet, profound and refreshing. 'Dew'* also suggests the falling of sleep upon the eyes.

[231] figures . . . fantasies *illusions of the fancy – 'figures' in the sense of 'shapes'*

[232] busy . . . draws *restless care conjures up*
Enter Portia *Her entrance is the more dramatic for its quietness. Her gently respectful words startle Brutus, lost in profound reflections on the health-giving power of sleep which is denied him (see p. 25). This theme is continued in their conversation, which is based on Plutarch's account.*

[234] what . . . you? *what do you want? Consider the tone of these questions.*

[235] commit *expose*

[236] weak condition *delicate constitution*

[237] ungently *discourteously*

[240] across *folded – the conventional sign of melancholy thoughts*

[245] Yet *Still*

[246] wafture *waving*

[249] enkindled *provoked*

[250] effect of humour *effect of some passing mood. It was thought that one's mood was determined by the predominance of one of the four humours in one's body – see note to V. v. 73-4.*

[251] sometime . . . hour *from time to time has a temporary effect on everyone*

BRUTUS Good gentlemen, look fresh and merrily.
        Let not our looks put on our purposes,
        But bear it as our Roman actors do,
        With untired spirits and formal constancy;
        And so good morrow to you everyone.
                          [*Exeunt all but* BRUTUS
        Boy! Lucius! Fast asleep? It is no matter,
        Enjoy the honey-heavy dew of slumber.   230
        Thou hast no figures nor no fantasies
        Which busy care draws in the brains of men;
        Therefore thou sleep'st so sound.

Enter PORTIA

PORTIA   Brutus, my lord.
BRUTUS Portia what mean you? Wherefore rise you
        now?
        It is not for your health thus to commit
        Your weak condition to the raw cold morning.
PORTIA Nor for yours neither. Y'have ungently,
        Brutus,
        Stole from my bed; and yesternight at supper
        You suddenly arose, and walked about,
        Musing and sighing, with your arms across;   240
        And when I asked you what the matter was,
        You stared upon me with ungentle looks.
        I urged you further; then you scratched your
        head,
        And too impatiently stamped with your foot;
        Yet I insisted, yet you answered not,
        But with an angry wafture of your hand
        Gave sign for me to leave you. So I did,
        Fearing to strengthen that impatience
        Which seemed too much enkindled, and
        withal
        Hoping it was but an effect of humour,   250
        Which sometime hath his hour with every man.

[253] work . . . shape *change your appearance as much*

[254] prevailed . . . condition *influenced your state of mind*

[255] Brutus *to be Brutus*

[256] your . . . grief *the cause of your distress*

[259] embrace . . . it *adopt the means to restore it. She tactfully points out that he has not told the truth.*

[261] physical *healthy – she has a demure persistence*

[262] unbraced *with doublet undone – see I. iii. 48.*

suck . . . humours *breathe in the dampness. The original meaning of 'humour' was 'moisture'.*

[263] What . . . sick? *She chides with gentle irony.*

[265] contagion . . . night *diseases carried on the night air*

[266] tempt . . . air *risk the damp air which causes catarrh, and is not yet purged of vapours by the sun*

[268] sick offence *harmful sickness*

[269] my place *as his wife*

[271] charm *implore – with the suggestion of using the magical power of her beauty*

[273] incorporate *make them one flesh*

[274] unfold *disclose*

your . . . half *a part of yourself, half of that unified being that our marriage made us*

[275] heavy *sad*

[276] Had resort *Visited*

[278] Even . . . darkness *Even from the darkness that made their disguise unnecessary. It is very human that she should keep back this conclusive evidence.*

[280–3] Within the bond . . . limitation *Dover Wilson has pointed out that the legal implications of the 'bond' of marriage are continued in a series of terms referring to land tenure: 'is it excepted' ('is an exception made in the agreement that . . .'), 'in sort' ('only in a particular manner') and 'limitation' ('for a limited period of time').*

[282] appertain *have reference*

[284] keep . . . you *keep you company*

[285–6] in . . . pleasure *in the outskirts of your affection, not in the heart. The London brothels were situated in the suburbs, leading on to l. 287. This speech follows Plutarch closely – ' "I . . . was married unto thee, not to be thy bed-fellow and companion in bed and at board only, like a harlot, but to be a partaker also with thee of thy good and evil fortune." '*

It will not let you eat, nor talk, nor sleep;
And could it work so much upon your shape,
As it hath much prevailed on your condition,
I should not know you Brutus. Dear my lord,
Make me acquainted with your case of grief.

BRUTUS I am not well in health, and that is all.

PORTIA Brutus is wise, and were he not in health
He would embrace the means to come by it.

BRUTUS Why, so I do. Good Portia, go to bed.   260

PORTIA Is Brutus sick, and is it physical
To walk unbraced and suck up the humours
Of the dank morning? What, is Brutus sick?
And will he steal out of his wholesome bed,
To dare the vile contagion of the night,
And tempt the rheumy and unpurgèd air
To add unto his sickness? No, my Brutus;
You have some sick offence within your mind,
Which, by the right and virtue of my place,
I ought to know of; and, upon my knees,   270
I charm you, by my once commended beauty,
By all your vows of love, and that great vow
Which did incorporate and make us one,
That you unfold to me, your self, your half,
Why you are heavy, and what men tonight
Have had resort to you; for here have been
Some six or seven, who did hide their faces
Even from darkness.

BRUTUS   Kneel not, gentle Portia.

PORTIA I should not need, if you were gentle Brutus.
Within the bond of marriage, tell me, Brutus, 280
Is it excepted I should know no secrets
That appertain to you? Am I your self
But, as it were, in sort or limitation,
To keep with you at meals, comfort your bed,
And talk to you sometimes? Dwell I but in the
    suburbs
Of your good pleasure? If it be no more,

[290] That . . . heart *It was thought that the blood was made in the liver and flowed from there to the heart, the supply being reduced in periods of stress or grief. The declaration is forced from Brutus, and is the more sincere for its simplicity.*

[292–302] I grant . . . secrets? *Another passage taken directly from Plutarch: having conceded that 'a woman's wit commonly is too weak to keep a secret safely', she continues ' "for myself, I have this benefit moreover that I am the daughter of Cato, and wife of Brutus. This notwithstanding, I did not trust to any of these things before, until that now I have found by experience that no pain or grief whatsoever can overcome me." With those words she showed him her wound on her thigh, and told him what she had done to prove herself. Brutus was amazed to hear what she said unto him, and lifting up his hands to heaven, he besought the gods to give him the grace he might bring his enterprise to so good pass, that he might be found a husband worthy of so noble a wife as Portia.'*

[292] withal *yet*

[295] Cato *Marcus Cato, orator and statesman, famous for his unbending Stoic morality. He fought for Pompey in the civil war, and after Pompey's death committed suicide at Utica to avoid capture by Caesar.*

[298] counsels *secret thoughts*

[299] strong . . . constancy *a severe test of my fortitude*

[305] thy . . . partake *thy heart shall share*

[307] engagements *commitments*
       construe *explain*

[308] charactery . . . brows *that is written on my brow, the meaning of its worried lines and wrinkles*

[312] stand aside *withdraw*
       how? *a form of greeting, 'How are things?'*

[313] Vouchsafe . . . morrow *Be so good as to accept my greeting of 'Good morning'*

Portia is Brutus' harlot, not his wife.

BRUTUS You are my true and honourable wife,
As dear to me as are the ruddy drops
That visit my sad heart.   290

PORTIA If this were true, then should I know this
secret.
I grant I am a woman; but withal
A woman that Lord Brutus took to wife.
I grant I am a woman; but withal
A woman well-reputed, Cato's daughter.
Think you I am no stronger than my sex,
Being so fathered, and so husbanded?
Tell me your counsels, I will not disclose 'em.
I have made strong proof of my constancy,
Giving myself a voluntary wound   300
Here, in the thigh. Can I bear that with
patience,
And not my husband's secrets?

BRUTUS   O ye gods,
Render me worthy of this noble wife!

Knocking within

Hark, hark! one knocks. Portia, go in awhile,
And by and by thy bosom shall partake
The secrets of my heart.
All my engagements I will construe to thee,
All the charactery of my sad brows.
Leave me with haste. [*Exit* PORTIA] Lucius,
who's that knocks?

Enter LUCIUS *with* LIGARIUS

LUCIUS Here is a sick man that would speak with you. 310
BRUTUS Caius Ligarius, that Metellus spake of.
Boy, stand aside. Caius Ligarius, how?
LIGARIUS Vouchsafe good morrow from a feeble
tongue.

[314] chose out *picked*
     brave *noble*

[315] wear a kerchief *be sick. It was common to protect one's head with a cloth in sickness.*

[319] Had . . . it *If you were healthy enough for it to be worth-while for me to tell you*

[321] I . . . sickness *He probably pulls off the kerchief.*

[322] Brave son *Noble son of Rome*

[323] exorcist *one who can control spirits, driving them from a sick man's body or summoning them by 'conjuring', using magical powers*

[324] mortified *dead. There is a pun on 'spirit'.*

[325] strive . . . impossible *attempt impossible things*

[326] What's to do? *What is to be done?*

[327] make . . . whole *restore to health those who suffer under Caesar's rule*

[330] unfold *disclose*

[331] To . . . done *The man whom we must 'make sick'*
     Set . . . foot *Proceed*

Thunder *Again the thunder underlines the resolution of the con-spirators (compare stage directions at I. iii. 100). The scene has raised doubts about Brutus's fitness as a leader, and has taken us deeply into his mind both in the soliloquies and in the intimate domestic episode with Portia; the conclusion restores his public image, ending the scene on a high note with Ligarius's magnificent tributes to him.*

ACT TWO, scene 2

The thunder links the two scenes as we move immediately from the murderers to their intended victim – there would be no curtain in the Elizabethan theatre – and recalls the omens of I. iii. that figure again in this scene.

night-gown *dressing-gown*

[2–3] Thrice hath . . . Caesar! *'He heard his wife Calphurnia, being fast asleep, weep and sigh, and put forth many fumbling lament-able speeches; for she dreamed that Caesar was slain.'* (Plutarch)

BRUTUS O what a time have you chose out, brave
    Caius,
    To wear a kerchief! Would you were not sick!
LIGARIUS I am not sick if Brutus have in hand
    Any exploit worthy the name of honour.
BRUTUS Such an exploit have I in hand, Ligarius,
    Had you a healthful ear to hear of it.
LIGARIUS By all the gods that Romans bow before,   320
    I here discard my sickness. Soul of Rome!
    Brave son, derived from honourable loins,
    Thou like an exorcist hast conjured up
    My mortified spirit. Now bid me run,
    And I will strive with things impossible,
    Yea, get the better of them. What's to do?
BRUTUS A piece of work that will make sick men
    whole.
LIGARIUS But are not some whole that we must make
    sick?
BRUTUS That must we also. What it is, my Caius,
    I shall unfold to thee as we are going   330
    To whom it must be done.
LIGARIUS   Set on your foot,
    And with a heart new-fired I follow you,
    To do I know not what; but it sufficeth
    That Brutus leads me on.
BRUTUS   Follow me then.

Thunder

[*Exeunt*

Scene 2. *Thunder and lightning. Enter* CAESAR *in his night-gown*

CAESAR Nor heaven nor earth have been at peace
    tonight.
    Thrice hath Calphurnia in her sleep cried out,

[3] Who's within   *a common formula for calling a servant*

[5] do . . . sacrifice   *sacrifice immediately*

[6] success   *result, whether the omens are good or bad*

[8] What . . . you?   *What do you intend? Calphurnia's agitated entrance contrasts with Portia's calm dignity. 'She prayed him . . . not to go out of doors that day, but to adjourn the session of the Senate until another day.' (Plutarch)*

[10] Caesar shall forth   *I shall go out. He uses the third person even to his wife.*

[11] Ne'er . . . back   *Only looked at my back*

[13] stood . . . ceremonies   *paid much attention to portents. 'Thereby it seemed that Caesar likewise did fear and suspect somewhat, because his wife . . . until that time was never given to any fear or superstition.' (Plutarch)*

[14] one within   *one of the household*

[16] horrid   *horrifying*

watch   *watchmen who patrolled the London streets at night. There were none in Caesar's Rome.*

[18–24] And graves . . . streets   *Shakespeare adds to the portents mentioned by Plutarch – the warriors may have been suggested by Josephus's account of the omens preceding the fall of Jerusalem. He recalled this passage in* Hamlet *(I. i. 113–20).*

[18] yawned . . . up   *opened and given up*

[20] right . . . war   *correct battle order*

[21] drizzled blood   *Dover Wilson relates this to the 'blood rain' common in south Europe. The focus of these portents is again the Capitol, symbol of Roman rule and the scene of the assassination (Compare I. iii. 20, 75, II. i. 111).*

[22] hurtled   *clashed*

[25] beyond . . . use   *beyond all normal experience*

'Help, ho! they murder Caesar!' Who's
within?

Enter a SERVANT

SERVANT My lord?
CAESAR Go bid the priests do present sacrifice,
　　　And bring me their opinions of success.
SERVANT I will, my lord.　　　　　　　　　[*Exit*

Enter CALPHURNIA

CALPHURNIA What mean you, Caesar? Think you to
　　　walk forth?
　　　You shall not stir out of your house today.
CAESAR Caesar shall forth. The things that threatened
　　　me　　　　　　　　　　　　　　　　　　10
　　　Ne'er looked but on my back; when they shall
　　　see
　　　The face of Caesar, they are vanished.
CALPHURNIA Caesar, I never stood on ceremonies,
　　　Yet now they fright me. There is one within,
　　　Besides the things that we have heard and
　　　seen,
　　　Recounts most horrid sights seen by the
　　　watch.
　　　A lioness hath whelped in the streets,
　　　And graves have yawned, and yielded up their
　　　dead;
　　　Fierce fiery warriors fought upon the clouds
　　　In ranks and squadrons and right form of war,　20
　　　Which drizzled blood upon the Capitol.
　　　The noise of battle hurtled in the air;
　　　Horses did neigh, and dying men did groan,
　　　And ghosts did shriek and squeal about the
　　　streets.
　　　O Caesar, these things are beyond all use,

[27] Whose . . . purposed *The outcome of which is predetermined*

[28] Yet *Still – in spite of these portents*

[29] Are . . . Caesar *Refer as much to the rest of the world as they do to Caesar*

[30] When . . . seen *The heavens do not predict the death of a common man*

[31] blaze forth *proclaim, with fiery comets and meteors*

[32] Cowards . . . deaths *in their imagination*

[33] never . . . once *experience death only once. 'And when some of his friends did counsel him to have a guard for the safety of his person . . . he would never consent to it, but said it was better to die once than always to be afraid of death.' (Plutarch) Is Caesar's speech noble or arrogant? It starts splendidly, but can he be sincere in expressing amazement that men should fear? Moreover, he still consults the augurs.*

[36] necessary *inevitable*

[37] augurers *augurs – see note to II. i. 200.*

[39] offering *animal sacrificed to the gods*

[40] They . . . beast *In Plutarch, Caesar was unable to find a heart in a beast he sacrificed himself on the previous day.*

[41] in . . . cowardice *to put cowards to shame*

[44–7] Danger . . . terrible *a rather empty and meaningless boast. Is Caesar finding it necessary to bolster his own determination?*

[46] littered *born*

[49] consumed in confidence *eaten up by self-confidence*

[50] Call . . . fear *She simultaneously suggests that he should do it to please her, and provides him with an excuse for the Senate.*

And I do fear them.

CAESAR   What can be avoided
Whose end is purposed by the mighty gods?
Yet Caesar shall go forth; for these pre-
dictions
Are to the world in general as to Caesar.

CALPHURNIA When beggars die, there are no comets
seen;   30
The heavens themselves blaze forth the death
of princes.

CAESAR Cowards die many times before their deaths;
The valiant never taste of death but once.
Of all the wonders that I yet have heard,
It seems to me most strange that men should
fear,
Seeing that death, a necessary end,
Will come when it will come.

Enter SERVANT

                  What say the augurers?

SERVANT They would not have you to stir forth
today.
Plucking the entrails of an offering forth,
They could not find a heart within the beast.   40

CAESAR The gods do this in shame of cowardice.
Caesar should be a beast without a heart
If he should stay at home today for fear.
No, Caesar shall not. Danger knows full well
That Caesar is more dangerous than he.
We are two lions littered in one day,
And I the elder and more terrible;
And Caesar shall go forth.

CALPHURNIA   Alas, my lord,
Your wisdom is consumed in confidence.
Do not go forth today. Call it my fear   50
That keeps you in the house, and not your own.

[54] prevail *overcome your objections*

[55] Mark . . . well '*When the soothsayers having sacrificed many beasts one after another, told him that none did like them, then he determined to send Antonius to adjourn the session of the Senate.*' (*Plutarch*)

[56] for . . . humour *to satisfy your whim. Caesar speaks indulgently.*

[59] fetch *conduct*

[60] in . . . time *at a most opportune moment*

[65] Say . . . sick *She is over-anxious and her hasty intervention is unfortunate: Caesar cannot acquiesce in a lie in front of Decius Brutus.*

[66] in . . . far *made such extensive conquests*

[67] greybeards *old men*

[68] will *strongly emphasised*

[70] Lest . . . so *subtly hinting that it is Caesar who will be laughed at, since Decius is only his messenger*

[71] The . . . will *There is no need for any other reason than that I have decided it*

[72] That . . . Senate *Caesar's contemptuous attitude to the Senate (see also l. 67) is perhaps the strongest evidence to support the conspirators' accusations of tyranny.*

[75] stays *keeps*

[76–9] She dreamt . . . it *Plutarch's account of the dream is different: '* the Senate having set upon the top of Caesar's house, for an ornament . . . , a certain pinnacle, Calphurnia dreamed that she saw it broken down*'. Shakespeare alters it to anticipate the manner of Caesar's death more closely (see III. i. 105–10; ii. 195–6) and to relate the dream symbolically to the themes of the play – see pp. 24–5.*

[76] tonight *last night*

      statue *pronounced as three syllables*

[78] lusty *vigorous*

[80] apply for *interpret as*

We'll send Mark Antony to the Senate House,
And he shall say you are not well today.
Let me upon my knee prevail in this.
CAESAR Mark Antony shall say I am not well,
And for thy humour I will stay at home.

Enter DECIUS

Here's Decius Brutus; he shall tell them so.
DECIUS Caesar, all hail! Good morrow, worthy Caesar.
I come to fetch you to the Senate House.
CAESAR And you are come in very happy time   60
To bear my greetings to the senators,
And tell them that I will not come today.
Cannot, is false; and that I dare not, falser;
I will not come today. Tell them so, Decius.
CALPHURNIA Say he is sick.
CAESAR   Shall Caesar send a lie?
Have I in conquest stretched mine arm so far
To be afeard to tell greybeards the truth?
Decius, go tell them Caesar will not come.
DECIUS Most mighty Caesar, let me know some
        cause,
Lest I be laughed at when I tell them so.   70
CAESAR The cause is in my will; I will not come;
That is enough to satisfy the Senate.
But for your private satisfaction,
Because I love you, I will let you know:
Calphurnia here, my wife, stays me at home.
She dreamt tonight she saw my statue,
Which like a fountain with an hundred spouts
Did run pure blood; and many lusty Romans
Came smiling, and did bathe their hands in it.
And these does she apply for warnings and
        portents   80
Of evils imminent; and on her knee
Hath begged that I will stay at home today.

97

[83] all amiss   *quite incorrectly*

[84] fair and fortunate   *promising good fortune*

[89] tinctures . . . cognizance   *These terms combine the miracu-lous powers of the relics of a saint with the honours bestowed by a prince in the form of coats of arms. 'Tinctures' (colours) are additions made to coats of arms, but with 'stains' and 'relics' suggest cloths dipped in blood, as the blood of martyrs was preserved; 'cog-nizances' are insignia worn by retainers.*

[91] well expounded it   *interpreted it correctly. Caesar is flat-tered by these comparisons.*

[92] I . . . say   *You will see that I have when you hear what else I can tell you*

[93–101] the Senate . . . afraid?   *Closely based on Plutarch: Decius 'laughed at the Soothsayers, and reproved Caesar, saying, "that he gave the Senate occasion to mislike with him, and that they might think he mocked them, considering that by his commandment they were assembled, and that they were ready . . . to proclaim him king of all his provinces of the Empire of Rome out of Italy . . . And, furthermore, that if any man should tell them from him they should depart for that present time, and return again when Calphurnia should have better dreams, what would his enemies and ill-willers say, and how could they like of his friends' words?"'*

[93] concluded   *decided*

[96–7] a mock . . . rendered   *a mocking jest likely to be made*

[102–3] my . . . proceeding   *my deep concern for your advance-ment*

[104] reason . . . liable   *prudence is overcome by my love. Decius has worked on three of Caesar's chief weaknesses — his wish for a crown, his fear of mockery (fatal to the inflated image he projects of himself), and his affectation that he cannot feel fear — and hastens to excuse himself for suggesting such criticisms.*

[108] fetch   *escort. Caesar turns cheerfully to express his apprecia-tion of Publius's courtesy. Cassius is noticeable by his absence.*

DECIUS This dream is all amiss interpreted;
         It was a vision fair and fortunate.
         Your statue spouting blood in many pipes,
         In which so many smiling Romans bathed,
         Signifies that from you great Rome shall suck
         Reviving blood, and that great men shall
            press
         For tinctures, stains, relics, and cognizance.
         This by Calphurnia's dream is signified.   90
CAESAR And this way have you well expounded it.
DECIUS I have, when you have heard what I can say;
         And know it now: the Senate have concluded
         To give this day a crown to mighty Caesar.
         If you shall send them word you will not
            come,
         Their minds may change. Besides, it were a
            mock
         Apt to be rendered for some one to say,
         'Break up the Senate till another time,
         When Caesar's wife shall meet with better
            dreams.'
         If Caesar hide himself, shall they not whisper,   100
         'Lo, Caesar is afraid'?
         Pardon me, Caesar, for my dear dear love
         To your proceeding bids me tell you this;
         And reason to my love is liable.
CAESAR How foolish do your fears seem now,
            Calphurnia!
         I am ashamed I did yield to them.
         Give me my robe, for I will go.

Enter PUBLIUS, BRUTUS, CASCA, CAIUS LIGARIUS, CINNA,
         METELLUS *and* TREBONIUS

         And look where Publius is come to fetch me.
PUBLIUS Good morrow Caesar.
CAESAR   Welcome Publius.

[111–13] Caius . . . lean   *Caesar has an affable word for all of them, but especially for his former enemy, simultaneously playing down their enmity and expressing sympathy for his sickness. Caius's leanness ominously recalls Caesar's comment on Cassius (I. ii. 194).*

[114] eight   *the hour at which the conspirators arranged to meet – another ominous note*

Enter Antony   *How do the conspirators react?*

[118] prepare within   *perhaps prepare the wine (l. 126)*

[120] Now   *a casually familiar greeting. Caesar shows himself 'consumed in confidence' – his courtesy might sway the audience's sympathies towards him, but it might seem the condescending hospitality of a dictator who is assured of his power and can afford to unbend.*

[127] like friends   *There is an ironic repetition of 'friends', and further irony in the word 'like'; being 'like friends' is not the same as 'being friends'.*

[128] That . . . same   *Brutus picks up the ambiguity in Caesar's words – to be 'like' something is not necessarily to be the same as that thing.*

[129] earns   *grieves*

Apart from one condescending remark (l. 105), Calphurnia has been ignored at the end of the scene. How does she behave through Decius's speeches and on the entry of the other conspirators?

ACT TWO, scene 3

Plutarch describes Artemidorus as 'a Doctor of Rhetoric in the Greek tongue, who by means of his profession was very familiar with certain of Brutus's confederates, and therefore knew the most part of all their practices against Caesar'. Shakespeare uses this episode to increase the tension before the murder – perhaps Caesar will be warned in time.

[2] have . . . to   *keep an eye on*

What, Brutus, are you stirred so early too?   110
Good morrow Casca. Caius Ligarius,
Caesar was ne'er so much your enemy
As that same ague which hath made you lean.
What is't o'clock?
BRUTUS   Caesar, 'tis strucken eight.
CAESAR I thank you for your pains and courtesy.

Enter ANTONY

See, Antony, that revels long a-nights,
Is notwithstanding up. Good morrow, Antony.
ANTONY So to most noble Caesar.
CAESAR   Bid them prepare within.
I am to blame to be thus waited for.
Now, Cinna; now, Metellus; what, Trebonius: 120
I have an hour's talk in store for you;
Remember that you call on me today;
Be near me, that I may remember you.
TREBONIUS Caesar, I will: [*Aside*] and so near will I be,
That your best friends shall wish I had been further.
CAESAR Good friends, go in, and taste some wine with me;
And we, like friends, will straightway go together.
BRUTUS [*Aside*] That every like is not the same, O Caesar,
The heart of Brutus earns to think upon.
               [*Exeunt*

Scene 3. *Enter* ARTEMIDORUS *reading a paper*

ARTEMIDORUS 'Caesar, beware of Brutus; take heed of Cassius; come not near Casca; have an eye to Cinna; trust not Trebonius; mark well Metellus Cimber;

[5–6] There . . . men *They have only one intention*

[6] bent *aimed – as a bow is bent*
[7] look . . . you *keep good watch*
[7–8] Security . . . conspiracy *Over-confidence (false security) opens a way for conspiracy to act*
[9] lover *dear friend*

[12] suitor *petitioner – someone presenting a 'suit'*

[13–14] virtue . . . emulation *virtue cannot live beyond the reach of envy's fangs*

[16] the Fates . . . contrive *destiny itself is conspiring to aid the traitors. The Fates in classical myth were three goddesses who spun the thread of man's destiny.*

ACT TWO, scene 4

The tension is further increased by Portia's agitation and the chance that her indiscretions will give the plot away. The audience's sympathies are again carefully balanced, her concern for Brutus complementing that of Artemidorus for Caesar. Plutarch says that 'being too weak to away with so great an inward grief of mind, she could hardly keep within, but was frighted with every little noise and cry she heard (ll. 16–19) . . . , asking every man that came from the market-place what Brutus did, and still sent messenger after messenger to know what news'.

[4] I . . . again *I would have liked you to have gone and returned*
[6] constancy . . . side *may my fortitude support me – compare II. i. 299. Her agitation contrasts sharply with her earlier confidence.*
[7] Set . . . tongue *to stop her expressing her feelings*
[9] counsel *secrets. Brutus has told her the plot in detail (see l. 15) as he promised (II. i. 305–8) – an audience would not notice that he has had no opportunity to do so.*
[10] yet *still*

Decius Brutus loves thee not; thou hast wronged
Caius Ligarius. There is but one mind in all these
men, and it is bent against Caesar. If thou beest not
immortal, look about you. Security gives way to
conspiracy. The mighty gods defend thee! Thy
lover,

Artemidorus.'   10

Here will I stand till Caesar pass along,
And as a suitor will I give him this.
My heart laments that virtue cannot live
Out of the teeth of emulation.
If thou read this, O Caesar, thou may'st live;
If not, the Fates with traitors do contrive.

[*Exit*

Scene 4. *Enter* PORTIA *and* LUCIUS

PORTIA I prithee, boy, run to the Senate House;
  Stay not to answer me, but get thee gone.
  Why dost thou stay?
LUCIUS   To know my errand, madam.
PORTIA I would have had thee there and here again
  Ere I can tell thee what thou shouldst do
    there.
  [*Aside*] O constancy, be strong upon my
    side;
  Set a huge mountain 'tween my heart and
    tongue.
  I have a man's mind, but a woman's might.
  How hard it is for women to keep counsel!
  [*To Lucius*] Art thou here yet?
LUCIUS   Madam, what should I do?   10
  Run to the Capitol, and nothing else?
  And so return to you, and nothing else?
PORTIA Yes, bring me word, boy, if thy lord look
    well,

[14] went . . . forth   *was sick when he went out*
take . . . note   *observe carefully*

[18] bustling rumour   *confused noise*
fray   *skirmish*
[20] Sooth   *Truly*

[23] ninth hour   *The passage of time towards the fatal hour is carefully marked (see II. ii. 114).*
[25] stand   *place*

[27] suit   *petition*

[29] To . . . Caesar   *To do himself a service*

[32] None . . . chance   *Nothing of which I am certain, much that I fear may happen*

[35] praetors   *magistrates*

[37] void   *empty*

PORTIA   For he went sickly forth; and take good
note
What Caesar doth, what suitors press to him.
Hark, boy, what noise is that?

LUCIUS I hear none, madam.

PORTIA   Prithee, listen well.
I heard a bustling rumour, like a fray,
And the wind brings it from the Capitol.

LUCIUS Sooth, madam, I hear nothing.   20

Enter the SOOTHSAYER

PORTIA Come hither, fellow. Which way hast thou
been?

SOOTHSAYER At mine own house, good lady.

PORTIA What is't a clock?

SOOTHSAYER   About the ninth hour, lady.

PORTIA Is Caesar yet gone to the Capitol?

SOOTHSAYER Madam, not yet; I go to take my stand,
To see him pass on to the Capitol.

PORTIA Thou hast some suit to Caesar, has thou
not?

SOOTHSAYER That I have, lady, if it will please Caesar
To be so good to Caesar as to hear me:
I shall beseech him to befriend himself.   30

PORTIA Why, know'st thou any harm's intended
towards him?

SOOTHSAYER None that I know will be, much that I
fear may chance.
Good morrow to you. Here the street is
narrow.
The throng that follows Caesar at the heels,
Of senators, of praetors, common suitors,
Will crowd a feeble man almost to death.
I'll get me to a place more void, and there
Speak to great Caesar as he comes along.

                                          [Exit

[41] speed   *assist*

[42-3] Brutus . . . grant   *Fearing that Lucius had heard her words she invents an innocent explanation of the 'enterprise'.*

[43] I . . . faint   *perhaps owing to her fear that the Soothsayer will succeed in warning Caesar, and his unintentional reference to the plan for the murder (ll. 34–6). Plutarch says that she fainted from the strain of waiting for Caesar's coming, and that Brutus was told that she was dying. Shakespeare alters the message that he is sent so that it is in accord with the dignity of her character.*

[44] commend me   *give my love*

[45] merry   *in good spirits*

PORTIA I must go in. Ay me, how weak a thing
The heart of woman is! O Brutus,   40
The heavens speed thee in thine enterprise.
[*Aside*] Sure, the boy heard me. [*To* LUCIUS]
   Brutus hath a suit
That Caesar will not grant. O, I grow faint.
Run Lucius, and commend me to my lord;
Say I am merry. Come to me again,
And bring me word what he doth say to
   thee.
                       [*Exeunt severally*

ACT THREE, scene 1

*Artemidorus and the Soothsayer station themselves as the
crowd gathers. The trumpet flourish shows that Caesar enters
ceremonially, closely attended by the conspirators.*

[1] The ides . . . come *from Plutarch – see p. 5. Caesar still
seems over-confident, yet he recognises the Soothsayer and remembers
his warning.*

[3] schedule *document*

[4–5] Trebonius . . . suit *This attempt to divert Caesar may
have been included in the plan as a precaution. Caesar knows of the
suit (see II. ii. 120–3), although it is the last we hear of it – Trebonius's
task is to draw Antony away (ll. 25–6).*

[4] o'er-read *read through*

[5] At . . . leisure *When it is most convenient to you*

[7] touches . . . nearer *is of more personal concern to Caesar*

[8] What . . . served *Artemidorus makes the same mistake as
Calphurnia of urging Caesar to act in public in a manner unworthy of
his reputation (II. ii. 65), and so prompts him to demonstrate his
magnanimity. Shakespeare's alteration of Plutarch (see p. 12) increases the drama of the episode – it is Caesar's character, not chance
circumstances, that prevents his receiving the warning.*

[10] What . . . mad *His desperation has provoked Artemidorus
into giving Caesar peremptory orders.*

Sirrah . . . place *Fellow, make way*

enter the Senate *This is not in the First Folio; there was no
need to indicate the precise location of scenes on the Elizabethan
stage. During the conversation that follows, Caesar would probably
mount a dais at the back of the stage, perhaps under the balcony.*

[18] makes to *makes his way to*

[19] be sudden *act promptly*

we . . . prevention *we fear we shall be forestalled*

[20–2] Brutus . . . myself *Cassius nearly panics; it is not even
certain that Popilius Lena refers to the conspiracy (although in
Plutarch he tells them that it is betrayed); it is striking that even in a
practical emergency Cassius turns for advice to Brutus.*

[21] turn back *return alive*

ACT THREE

Scene I. *A crowd, among them* ARTEMIDORUS *and the*
SOOTHSAYER. *Flourish. Enter* CAESAR, BRUTUS,
CASSIUS, CASCA, DECIUS, METELLUS CIMBER, TRE-
BONIUS, CINNA, ANTONY, LEPIDUS, POPILIUS,
PUBLIUS

CAESAR The ides of March are come.
SOOTHSAYER Ay, Caesar, but not gone.
ARTEMIDORUS Hail, Caesar! Read this schedule.
DECIUS Trebonius doth desire you to o'er-read,
    At your best leisure, this his humble suit.
ARTEMIDORUS O Caesar, read mine first; for mine's a
    suit
        That touches Caesar nearer. Read it, great
        Caesar.
CAESAR What touches us ourself shall be last served.
ARTEMIDORUS Delay not, Caesar, read it instantly.
CAESAR What, is the fellow mad?
PUBLIUS   Sirrah, give place.   10
CASSIUS What, urge you your petitions in the street?
    Come to the Capitol.

              CAESAR *and the rest enter the Senate*

POPILIUS I wish your enterprise today may thrive.
CASSIUS What enterprise, Popilius?
POPILIUS   Fare you well.
BRUTUS What said Popilius Lena?
CASSIUS He wished today our enterprise might thrive.
    I fear our purpose is discovered.
BRUTUS Look how he makes to Caesar. Mark him.
CASSIUS Casca, be sudden, for we fear prevention.
    Brutus, what shall be done? If this be known,   20
    Cassius or Caesar never shall turn back,
    For I will slay myself.

[22] be constant *control yourself*

[24] change *change his expression*

[25] knows his time *when he should act*

[28] presently prefer *at once present*

[29] addressed *ready*
second *support*

[30] rears *raises. Casca moves behind Caesar.*

[32] Caesar . . . senate *Caesar speaks as if he were a king and the Senate the ministers he has appointed.*

redress *put right. Caesar's use of the word might recall, ironically, the conspirators' determination to gain redress by his death (see II. i. 55–8).*

[33] puissant *powerful*

[34] seat *'Throne' is implied. He addresses Caesar with extravagantly servile flattery, as if he were a tyrant.*

[35] prevent *forestall*

[36] couchings . . . courtesies *prostrations and grovelling obeisances*

[37] fire.the blood *inflame the pride*

[38–9] turn . . . children *change fundamental and primary laws into the rules for children's games. 'Law' is Johnson's emendation of the Folio's 'lane' – which might possibly be used in the sense of 'ways'.*

[39–40] fond/To *so foolish as to*

[40] bears . . . rebel *so unstable – divided within himself*

[41] thawed . . . quality *changed from the virtue it ought to have – that Caesar's single-minded determination can be softened, made malleable like a base metal*

[42] melteth *persuades, mollifies*

[43] Low . . . curtsies *Obeisances on humbly bended knee*

base . . . fawning *cringing like a spaniel that wants to be petted. Shakespeare often associates flattery with fawning dogs and images of melting and sweetness.*

[46] spurn . . . cur *kick you like a dog. 'Caesar . . . perceiving they still pressed on him, he violently thrust them from him'. (Plutarch)*

[47–8] Caesar . . . satisfied *Caesar does not act unjustly, nor will he be convinced without good reason. Ben Jonson accused Shakespeare of writing the absurd line 'Caesar did never wrong, but with just cause' – either Jonson remembered it incorrectly, or Shakespeare altered the line because of this criticism.*

BRUTUS   Cassius, be constant.
    Popilius Lena speaks not of our purposes,
    For look, he smiles, and Caesar doth not
      change.
CASSIUS Trebonius knows his time; for look you,
      Brutus,
    He draws Mark Antony out of the way.
                  [*Exeunt* ANTONY *and* TREBONIUS
DECIUS Where is Metellus Cimber? Let him go,
    And presently prefer his suit to Caesar.
BRUTUS He is addressed; press near and second him.
CINNA Casca, you are the first that rears your hand.   30
CAESAR Are we all ready? What is now amiss
    That Caesar and his senate must redress?
METELLUS Most high, most mighty, and most
      puissant Caesar,
    Metellus Cimber throws before thy seat
    An humble heart –

Kneeling

CAESAR   I must prevent thee, Cimber.
    These couchings and these lowly courtesies
    Might fire the blood of ordinary men,
    And turn pre-ordinance and first decree
    Into the law of children. Be not fond
    To think that Caesar bears such rebel blood   40
    That will be thawed from the true quality
    With that which melteth fools: I mean sweet
      words,
    Low-crooked curtsies, and base spaniel fawn-
      ing.
    Thy brother by decree is banishèd:
    If thou dost bend and pray and fawn for him,
    I spurn thee like a cur out of my way.
    Know, Caesar doth not wrong, nor without
      cause
    Will he be satisfied.

[51] **repealing** *recall from exile*

[54] **freedom of repeal** *permission to be recalled*

[55] **What, Brutus?** *He is surprised that Brutus should oppose him.*

[57] **enfranchisement** *restoration of rights of citizenship*

[58–9] **I . . . me** *I might well be persuaded if I were like you; if like you I could bring myself to plead with others to change their minds, then pleas might influence me*

[60] **constant . . . star** *as unchanging as the pole star – round which the other stars move*

[61] **true . . . quality** *immovable and stable quality*

[62] **fellow . . . firmament** *equal in the heavens*

[63] **unnumbered** *innumerable*

[65] **but . . . place** *only one that keeps its position. Caesar expands on the idea, spelling it out self-indulgently – yet he silences the conspirators.*

[66] **furnished well** *well supplied*

[67] **apprehensive** *possessed of reason*

[69] **unassailable . . . rank** *keeps his position without fear of attack. There is grim irony in his words.*

[70] **Unshaked of motion** *Undisturbed by external influences. Motion' here combines this sense of the word (as in ll. 58–9) with the physical motion of the stars.*

[74] **Lift up Olympus** *attempt the impossible. The Greek mountain, Olympus, was reputed to be the home of the gods, with whom Caesar is comparing himself.*

[75] **bootless** *uselessly – implying that if Brutus's plea is unavailing, then no one can hope to succeed*

[76] **Speak . . . me!** *Let the action of my hands express my opinion!*

METELLUS Is there no voice more worthy than my
    own,
    To sound more sweetly in great Caesar's ear   50
    For the repealing of my banished brother?
BRUTUS I kiss thy hand, but not in flattery, Caesar;
    Desiring thee that Publius Cimber may
    Have an immediate freedom of repeal.
CAESAR What, Brutus?
CASSIUS   Pardon, Caesar; Caesar, pardon:
    As low as to thy foot doth Cassius fall,
    To beg enfranchisement for Publius Cimber.
CAESAR I could be well moved, if I were as you;
    If I could pray to move, prayers would move
    me;
    But I am constant as the northern star,   60
    Of whose true-fixed and resting quality
    There is no fellow in the firmament.
    The skies are painted with unnumbered
    sparks,
    They are all fire, and every one doth shine;
    But there's but one in all doth hold his place.
    So in the world: 'tis furnished well with
    men,
    And men are flesh and blood, and
    apprehensive;
    Yet in the number I do know but one
    That unassailable holds on his rank,
    Unshaked of motion; and that I am he,   70
    Let me a little show it, even in this,
    That I was constant Cimber should be
    banished,
    And constant do remain to keep him so.
CINNA O Caesar –
CAESAR   Hence! Wilt thou lift up Olympus?
DECIUS Great Caesar –
CAESAR   Doth not Brutus bootless kneel?
CASCA Speak hands for me!

They stab Caesar   *first Casca from behind, followed by the others as Caesar tries to defend himself*

[77] Et tu, Brute?   *Even you, Brutus?* '*Brute' is pronounced as two syllables. This phrase had become traditional; it derives from the words attributed to Caesar by Suetonius, 'And thou, my son?', referring to his belief that Brutus was his illegitimate son.*

      Then . . . Caesar   *If Brutus strikes at him, that is the end.* '*Caesar did still defend himself against the rest . . . but when he saw Brutus with his sword drawn in his hand, then he pulled his gown over his head, and made no more resistance.' (Plutarch)*

[80] common pulpits   *public platforms for orators. Shakespeare may be thinking of the open-air pulpits in London.*

[83] Ambition's . . . paid   *Ambition has received its deserts*

[85] Publius   *an aged senator, too feeble to fly*

[86] confounded . . . mutiny   *stupefied by the uproar*

[87] fast   *close, firmly together*

[89] Talk . . . standing   *This is no time to consider standing on the defensive*

      good cheer   *be at ease. Brutus shows both consideration for Publius and astuteness in using his authority to calm the people.*

[93] mischief   *injury*

[94] abide   *bear the consequences for*

[96] amazed   *utterly astounded*

[97] wives   *women*

[98] As . . . doomsday   *As if it were the Day of Judgement*

[98–121] Fates . . . Rome   *The murder has left them in a certain state of shock and they talk with heady elation. Even Brutus indulges in flamboyant rhetoric more characteristic of Cassius.*

[98] Fates . . . pleasures   *We wish to know what destiny fate pleases to give us – see note to II. iii. 16.*

[99–100] 'tis . . . upon   *it is only when they are to die, and how to prolong their days, that men are concerned about*

[101–2] Why, he . . . death   *a typically cynical comment, and – for the audience – an ironic echo of Caesar's words (II. ii. 35–7)*

They stab CAESAR

CAESAR Et tu, Brute? Then fall, Caesar!

[*Dies*

CINNA Liberty! Freedom! Tyranny is dead!
　　　Run hence, proclaim, cry it about the streets.
CASSIUS Some to the common pulpits, and cry out,　80
　　　'Liberty, freedom, and enfranchisement!'
BRUTUS People and senators, be not affrighted.
　　　Fly not; stand still. Ambition's debt is paid.
CASCA Go to the pulpit, Brutus.
DECIUS 　　　　　　　　　And Cassius too.
BRUTUS Where's Publius?
CINNA Here, quite confounded with this mutiny.
METELLUS Stand fast together, lest some friend of
　　　　Caesar's
　　　Should chance –
BRUTUS Talk not of standing. Publius, good cheer;
　　　There is no harm intended to your person,　90
　　　Nor to no Roman else. So tell them, Publius.
CASSIUS And leave us, Publius, lest that the people,
　　　Rushing on us, should do your age some
　　　　mischief.
BRUTUS Do so; and let no man abide this deed
　　　But we the doers.

Enter TREBONIUS

CASSIUS Where is Antony?
TREBONIUS 　　　　　　　Fled to his house amazed.
　　　Men, wives, and children stare, cry out, and run,
　　　As it were doomsday.
BRUTUS 　　　　　　Fates, we will know your pleasures.
　　　That we shall die, we know; 'tis but the
　　　　time,
　　　And drawing days out, that men stand upon.　100
CASCA Why, he that cuts off twenty years of life
　　　Cuts off so many years of fearing death.

[103] Grant that   *If you agree to that – Brutus continues Casca's cynical train of thought. It has been argued that he treats it as a serious philosophical reflection, but this is a strangely unfeeling comment on the murder of a man he esteemed so highly.*

[105–10] Stoop . . . liberty   *Brutus intends this as a ritual gesture, showing them to be 'sacrificers' and not 'butchers' (II. i. 166), but it is ironical that he should urge them to cry 'Peace' while waving bloodstained weapons – even if it is a tyrant's blood (see pp. 17–18).*

[112] lofty scene   *noble action*

[113] states . . . unknown   *states not yet founded and languages which are as yet unknown – i.e. their fame will last for centuries and spread through the whole world*

[114] in sport   *for entertainment – as is happening as these words are spoken in the theatre*

[115] Pompey's basis   *the pedestal of Pompey's statue. The murder took place in Pompey's theatre (see III. ii. 195).*

along   *stretched out*

[117] knot   *group of conspirators bound closely together*

[119] shall . . . forth   *shall we go out*

[120] grace . . . heels   *honour him by following*

[121] most . . . best   *The double superlative was commonly used to give additional emphasis.*

[122] Soft   *Wait a moment. They are pulled up short by this entrance, which begins the counter-action that will destroy them. The tone of the scene changes dramatically (see p. 10). The Servant has been precisely instructed (l. 125); one hears Antony's voice in the circumspect, ambiguous language and carefully balanced statements that mark his public oratory, and by means of which he now treads a knife-edge between appearing hypocritical and antagonising his suspicious enemies. In Plutarch Antony invited the conspirators to leave the Senate, sending his son as a hostage, but did not meet them until the next day. Shakespeare adds this episode to tighten the action and to show Antony's mastery of the situation.*

[126] honest   *honourable*

[127] royal   *magnanimous – with a suggestion of his aspirations to kingship*

[129] feared   *tactfully implying that his loyalty to Caesar was partly due to fear*

BRUTUS Grant that, and then is death a benefit;
    So are we Caesar's friends, that have abridged
    His time of fearing death. Stoop Romans,
        stoop,
    And let us bathe our hands in Caesar's blood
    Up to the elbows, and besmear our swords;
    Then walk we forth, even to the market place,
    And waving our red weapons o'er our heads,
    Let's all cry, 'Peace, freedom, and liberty!'   110
CASSIUS Stoop then, and wash. How many ages
        hence
    Shall this our lofty scene be acted over,
    In states unborn, and accents yet unknown.
BRUTUS How many times shall Caesar bleed in sport,
    That now on Pompey's basis lies along,
    No worthier than the dust.
CASSIUS   So oft as that shall be,
    So often shall the knot of us be called
    The men that gave their country liberty.
DECIUS What, shall we forth?
CASSIUS   Ay, every man away.
    Brutus shall lead, and we will grace his heels   120
    With the most boldest and best hearts of
        Rome.

Enter a SERVANT

BRUTUS Soft, who comes here? A friend of Antony's.
SERVANT Thus, Brutus, did my master bid me
        kneel;
    Thus did Mark Antony bid me fall down,
    And, being prostrate, thus he bade me say:
    Brutus is noble, wise, valiant, and honest;
    Caesar was mighty, bold, royal, and loving.
    Say I love Brutus, and I honour him;
    Say I feared Caesar, honoured him, and loved
        him.

[130] vouchsafe   *graciously permit*

[131] resolved   *have explained to him*

[136] untrod state   *new and unknown state of affairs*

[137] all . . . faith   *complete loyalty*

[140] so . . . come   *if it pleases him to come*

[141] satisfied   *given an explanation*

[142] presently   *immediately*

[143] well to friend   *as a good friend*

[144] mind   *presentiment*

[145–6] still . . . purpose   *always turns out to be disagreeably accurate*

[148] O mighty Caesar!   *Antony goes straight to Caesar, ignoring Brutus's welcome. He expresses his genuine love for Caesar, but this is also a bold move to ensure his safety – he knows that Brutus will sympathise with this display of loyalty.*

[150] this . . . measure   *the area covered by his dead body*

[152] let blood   *killed. The euphemism refers to the common medical practice of bleeding a patient (compare II. i. 180).*

  rank   *both 'overgrown' (and so too powerful) and 'corrupted by disease', continuing the medical metaphor*

[153–63] If I . . . age   *Brutus has promised his safety – see lines 141–2 and note to l. 148. Already Antony has taken the initiative and establishes his moral superiority.*

[155] Of . . . as   *Of half the worth of*

[157] bear me hard   *bear enmity against me*

[158] purpled   *dark red with blood*

  smoke   *steam*

If Brutus will vouchsafe that Antony   130
May safely come to him, and be resolved
How Caesar hath deserved to lie in death,
Mark Antony shall not love Caesar dead
So well as Brutus living; but will follow
The fortunes and affairs of noble Brutus
Thorough the hazards of this untrod state
With all true faith. So says my master Antony.

BRUTUS   Thy master is a wise and valiant Roman;
    I never thought him worse.
    Tell him, so please him come unto this place,   140
    He shall be satisfied; and, by my honour,
    Depart untouched.

SERVANT   I'll fetch him presently.
                                   [Exit

BRUTUS   I know that we shall have him well to friend.

CASSIUS   I wish we may. But yet have I a mind
    That fears him much; and my misgiving still
    Falls shrewdly to the purpose.

Enter ANTONY

BRUTUS   But here comes Antony. Welcome, Mark
    Antony.

ANTONY   O mighty Caesar! Dost thou lie so low?
    Are all thy conquests, glories, triumphs, spoils,
    Shrunk to this little measure? Fare thee well.   150
    I know not, gentlemen, what you intend,
    Who else must be let blood, who else is rank;
    If I myself, there is no hour so fit
    As Caesar's death hour, nor no instrument
    Of half that worth as those your swords, made
      rich
    With the most noble blood of all this world.
    I do beseech ye, if you bear me hard,
    Now, whilst your purpled hands do reek and
      smoke,

[159] Fulfil ... pleasure *Complete the fulfilment of your desires. He implies that they enjoy murder.*

      Live *If I live*

[160] apt *ready*

[161] mean *means*

[163] choice ... spirits *most distinguished men and controlling geniuses – doubtless ironic*

[166] by our hands *Brutus must now recognise that the effect of his ritual action is to make them look like butchers.*

      our ... act *the act of murder we have now committed*

[168] bleeding business *act of bloodshed. The phrase deprives it of any dignity.*

[169] pitiful *full of pity*

[170] to ... Rome *for the injustice suffered by the whole of Rome*

[171] As ... fire *As one fire puts out another – proverbial*

      pity pity *pity for Rome drives out pity for Caesar*

[173] have ... points *are harmless*

[174] in ... malice *Many attempts have been made to emend this phrase, but it makes sense if it is taken to mean 'which appear to be strongly hostile' – continuing the contrast between the murderous appearance of their hands and the benevolent feelings in their hearts.*

[175] Of ... temper *Softened by brotherly love*

      receive you in *welcome you as one of us*

[177] Your ... strong *Your vote will be as influential*

[178] disposing ... dignities *distribution of new honours and appointments to offices of state. Brutus offers brotherly love; Cassius a share in the power.*

[181] deliver you *make known to you*

[183] proceeded *acted*

      I ... wisdom *Antony refers to their wisdom, an ambiguous word, rather than their good intentions.*

[184] Let ... hand *A parody of Brutus's handshaking (II. i. 112), with irony hinted by Antony's continued insistence that they are 'bloody' hands. He faces each in turn, and, as several commentators have remarked, marks each down for revenge.*

[188] my ... Casca *an ironic allusion to the fact that Casca struck Caesar from behind*

Fulfil your pleasure. Live a thousand years,
I shall not find myself so apt to die; 160
No place will please me so, no mean of death,
As here by Caesar, and by you cut off,
The choice and master spirits of this age.

BRUTUS O Antony, beg not your death of us.
Though now we must appear bloody and
  cruel,
As by our hands and this our present act
You see we do; yet see you but our hands,
And this the bleeding business they have done.
Our hearts you see not, they are pitiful;
And pity to the general wrong of Rome – 170
As fire drives out fire, so pity pity –
Hath done this deed on Caesar. For your part,
To you our swords have leaden points, Mark
  Antony;
Our arms, in strength of malice, and our
  hearts
Of brothers' temper, do receive you in
With all kind love, good thoughts, and
  reverence.

CASSIUS Your voice shall be as strong as any man's
In the disposing of new dignities.

BRUTUS Only be patient till we have appeased
The multitude, beside themselves with fear, 180
And then we will deliver you the cause,
Why I, that did love Caesar when I struck
  him,
Have thus proceeded.

ANTONY   I doubt not of your wisdom.
Let each man render me his bloody hand.
First, Marcus Brutus, will I shake with you;
Next, Caius Cassius, do I take your hand;
Now, Decius Brutus, yours; now yours,
  Metellus;
Yours, Cinna; and, my valiant Casca, yours;

[189] Though . . . Trebonius *It was Trebonius who drew Antony away so that he could not help Caesar.*

[190] Gentlemen all *The pause points the irony.*

[191] My . . . ground *My reputation is now so unstable – perhaps with an allusion to the blood-stained ground*

[192] conceit *consider*

[196] dearer *more keenly*

[199] Most noble *either addressing Caesar, or an ironic reference to the conspirators*

　　　corse *corpse*

[202] close *come to an agreement*

[204] bayed *brought to bay, like a hunted animal*

　　　hart *deer. 'Heart' is also implied, and the pun becomes explicit in l. 208.*

[206] Signed . . . spoil *Marked with your blood, which they have shared between them. The 'spoil' was the killing of the animal and its division between the hounds. The image recalls Brutus's distinction between sacrificial killing – carving Caesar as a dish for the gods, as a deer should be killed – and hewing him for the hounds (II. i. 173–4), and implies that staining their hands with blood – which Brutus intended as part of the sacrificial ritual – in fact shows that they took the latter line of action.*

　　　lethe *death. Lethe (pronounced as two syllables) was a river of the underworld; if one drank its water one forgot the past, hence the word came to mean 'oblivion'.*

[207] O . . . hart *The whole world was Caesar's natural realm*

[209] How . . . princes *Antony preserves his careful balance combining praise of Caesar with flattery of his murderers.*

[211–13] Mark Antony . . . modesty *He anticipates Cassius's protest at this tribute to Caesar and neatly turns it away.*

[213] cold modesty *calm understatement*

[215] compact *agreement*

[216] pricked *marked on the list – see IV. i. 1.*

[217] on . . . you *proceed without reckoning on your support*

Though last, not least in love, yours, good
  Trebonius.
Gentlemen all – alas, what shall I say?   190
My credit now stands on such slippery
  ground
That one of two bad ways you must conceit
  me,
Either a coward, or a flatterer.
That I did love thee, Caesar, O 'tis true.
If then thy spirit look upon us now,
Shall it not grieve thee dearer than thy death
To see thy Antony making his peace,
Shaking the bloody fingers of thy foes,
Most noble, in the presence of thy corse?
Had I as many eyes as thou hast wounds,   200
Weeping as fast as they stream forth thy
  blood,
It would become me better than to close
In terms of friendship with thine enemies.
Pardon me, Julius! Here wast thou bayed,
  brave hart;
Here didst thou fall; and here thy hunters
  stand,
Signed in thy spoil, and crimsoned in thy
  lethe.
O world, thou wast the forest to this hart;
And this, indeed, O world, the heart of thee.
How like a deer, strucken by many princes,
Dost thou here lie.   210
CASSIUS Mark Antony –
ANTONY   Pardon me, Caius Cassius,
The enemies of Caesar shall say this;
Then, in a friend, it is cold modesty.
CASSIUS I blame you not for praising Caesar so;
But what compact mean you to have with us?
Will you be pricked in number of our friends,
Or shall we on, and not depend on you?

JULIUS CAESAR

[218] Therefore   *To indicate that*

[219] Swayed   *Diverted*

[221] Upon . . . hope   *In the hope that*

[223] Or else   *If we did not give you reasons*

[224] good regard   *sound considerations*

[225] son of Caesar   *This may be an allusion to the rumour that Brutus was Caesar's illegitimate son.*

[227] am . . . suitor   *in addition would request. For Antony this is the vital point, but 'moreover' suggests that it is merely an afterthought.*

[228] Produce   *Bring forth*

[229] pulpit   *See note to l. 80.*

[230] order   *ceremony*

[231–5] Brutus . . . utter?   *Cassius speaks urgently*

[235] By . . . pardon   *Pardon me for contradicting you. Brutus is blandly complacent about the rightness of their cause and his own powers to convince the crowd of this by 'reason'. Cassius is overruled for the fourth time; Plutarch describes this as Brutus's 'second fault . . . which indeed marred all', and reports that Cassius 'spoke stoutly against it'.*

[237] our Caesar's   *This affectionate way of speaking of Caesar shows his confidence; as they have nothing to fear he can afford to be generous.*

[238] protest   *proclaim*

[240–2] Caesar shall . . . wrong   *These were the arguments Antony used – in the Senate – for giving Caesar a public funeral 'thinking good his testament should be read openly, and also that his body should be honourably buried, and not in huggermugger, lest the people might thereby take occasion to be worse offended if they did otherwise'. (Plutarch)*

[242] advantage . . . wrong   *benefit more than harm us*

[243] fall   *happen*

[246] devise   *think up*

ANTONY Therefore I took your hands, but was indeed
      Swayed from the point by looking down on
        Caesar.
      Friends am I with you all, and love you all,   220
      Upon this hope, that you shall give me
        reasons
      Why, and wherein, Caesar was dangerous.
BRUTUS Or else were this a savage spectacle.
      Our reasons are so full of good regard,
      That were you, Antony, the son of Caesar,
      You should be satisfied.
ANTONY   That's all I seek;
      And am moreover suitor that I may
      Produce his body to the market place,
      And in the pulpit, as becomes a friend,
      Speak in the order of his funeral.   230
BRUTUS You shall, Mark Antony.
CASSIUS   Brutus, a word with you.
      [*Aside to* BRUTUS] You know not what you do.
        Do not consent
      That Antony speak in his funeral.
      Know you how much the people may be
        moved
      By that which he will utter?
BRUTUS   By your pardon;
      I will myself into the pulpit first,
      And show the reason of our Caesar's death.
      What Antony shall speak, I will protest
      He speaks by leave, and by permission;
      And that we are contented Caesar shall   240
      Have all true rites and lawful ceremonies.
      It shall advantage more than do us wrong.
CASSIUS I know not what may fall; I like it not.
BRUTUS Mark Antony, here take you Caesar's body.
      You shall not in your funeral speech blame
        us,
      But speak all good you can devise of Caesar,

[249–51] And you . . . ended *Brutus's egotism becomes somewhat distasteful.*

[251–2] Be . . . more *This simple statement sounds humbly compliant, but it also expresses his complete assurance of success.*

[254–75] O pardon . . . burial *Consider how Antony might effect the transition from his cautious dealings with the conspirators to this emotional outburst. While he reveals the full horror of the murder, our sympathy for his genuine grief may be tempered by its savagery – he seems to relish the devastation that he prophesies.*

[255] butchers *Compare II. i. 166.*

[256] ruins *remains*

[257] tide of times *stream of history*

[258] costly blood *blood that is precious and that will be dearly paid for by the conspirators*

[260] like . . . mouths *The wounds seem to be pleading for revenge (see III. ii. 232–3).*

[261] To . . . tongue *To beg my voice and tongue to speak for them*

[262] light *fall*

[263] Domestic fury *Internal strife*

[264] cumber *burden*

[265] in use *customary*

[268] quartered . . . war *cut to pieces by warlike hands*

[269] choked . . . deeds *stifled by familiarity with cruel deeds*

[270] Caesar's spirit *implying a further reflection on the failure of Brutus's ideals. He has failed to 'come by' Caesar's spirit (see p. 18) and it haunts him and Cassius to the end of the play (see p. 13).*

ranging *scouring the earth for its prey*

[271] Ate *the Greek goddess of discord and destruction – pronounced as two syllables*

[272] confines *regions*

[273] havoc *no quarter. To 'cry havoc' was to order the slaughter and pillage of a defeated enemy, an order that only a king could give.*

let slip *unleash*

dogs of war *They are identified in Henry V, I. Chorus, 6–8 as famine, sword, and fire.*

[275] carrion *dead – see note to II. i. 130.*

And say you do't by our permission;
Else shall you not have any hand at all
About his funeral. And you shall speak
In the same pulpit whereto I am going,   250
After my speech is ended.

ANTONY   Be it so;
I do desire no more.

BRUTUS Prepare the body then, and follow us.

                    [*Exeunt all but* ANTONY

ANTONY O pardon me, thou bleeding piece of earth,
That I am meek and gentle with these
     butchers.
Thou art the ruins of the noblest man
That ever lived in the tide of times.
Woe to the hand that shed this costly blood!
Over thy wounds now do I prophesy –
Which like dumb mouths do ope their ruby
     lips,   260
To beg the voice and utterance of my
     tongue –
A curse shall light upon the limbs of men;
Domestic fury and fierce civil strife
Shall cumber all the parts of Italy;
Blood and destruction shall be so in use,
And dreadful objects so familiar,
That mothers shall but smile when they
     behold
Their infants quartered with the hands of
     war,
All pity choked with custom of fell deeds;
And Caesar's spirit, ranging for revenge,   270
With Ate by his side come hot from hell,
Shall in these confines with a monarch's voice
Cry havoc, and let slip the dogs of war,
That this foul deed shall smell above the
     earth
With carrion men, groaning for burial.

[281] O Caesar! *He sees the body.*
[282] big *swollen with grief*
[283] Passion *Grief*
[287] Post *Ride fast*
    chanced *happened*
[289] Rome *There is again a pun on 'Rome' and 'room'.*
[290] Hie *Hasten*
[291] back *return*
[292] try *test*
[294] cruel issue *the result of the cruelty – with perhaps a suggestion of an issue of blood. The legal associations of 'issue' link it with 'try' (l. 292).*
[295] the which *how the people take it*
    discourse *describe*
[297] Lend . . . hand *to help carry the body off – necessary as there were no curtains on the Elizabethan stage*

ACT THREE, scene 2

The crowd is in an uneasy and threatening mood.

[1] satisfied *given a satisfactory explanation*
[2] audience *a hearing*

[4] part the numbers *divide the crowd*

Enter a SERVANT

You serve Octavius Caesar, do you not?
SERVANT I do, Mark Antony.
ANTONY Caesar did write for him to come to Rome.
SERVANT He did receive his letters, and is coming,
    And bid me say to you by word of mouth –   280
    O Caesar!
ANTONY Thy heart is big; get thee apart and weep.
    Passion, I see, is catching, for mine eyes,
    Seeing those beads of sorrow stand in thine,
    Began to water. Is thy master coming?
SERVANT He lies tonight within seven leagues of
    Rome.
ANTONY Post back with speed, and tell him what hath
    chanced.
    Here is a mourning Rome, a dangerous Rome,
    No Rome of safety for Octavius yet;
    Hie hence, and tell him so. Yet stay awhile,   290
    Thou shalt not back till I have borne this
    corse
    Into the market place. There shall I try
    In my oration, how the people take
    The cruel issue of these bloody men;
    According to the which, thou shalt discourse
    To young Octavius of the state of things.
    Lend me your hand.
                  [Exeunt with CAESAR'S *body*

Scene 2. *Enter* BRUTUS *and* CASSIUS, *and* CITIZENS

CITIZENS We will be satisfied; let us be satisfied.
BRUTUS Then follow me, and give me audience,
    friends.
    Cassius, go you into the other street,
    And part the numbers.

[7] **public reasons** *reasons concerning the public good*

[10] **severally** *separately. It sounds as if the crowd is prepared to consider the question rationally.*

[12] **last** *end of his speech*

[13-36] **Romans ... reply** *Brutus's speech is formal and academic, modelled on Plutarch's description of his style (see p. 6) and developed in the balanced, antithetical manner popular at the end of the sixteenth century. It demands the close attention from the audience which he requests (ll. 13-18). As he appeals to reason, the speech is in prose, but he offers no evidence for his charges against Caesar, relying on his conviction of the rightness of his cause, on the power of his own reputation to sway the crowd, and on their response, as Romans, to the abstract ideals of honour, liberty and patriotism.*

[13] **Romans ... lovers** *The terms become increasingly personal – 'Romans' invokes the virtues expected of a Roman.*

    lovers *dear friends*

[13-18] **hear ... judge** *an intricate pattern. The sentences are of parallel form, and the end of each repeats its beginning.*

[13-14] **for my cause** *for the sake of the cause that I represent*

[15] **respect to** *regard for*

[17] **awake ... senses** *let your reason (good sense) be alert. He speaks in a rather 'schoolmasterly' way.*

[18-23] **If there ... more** *two more parallel sentences; there is a little more progression in the argument, but only to assert Brutus's own position in the concluding antithesis. He rationalises the issues with which he struggled earlier into too simple a formula.*

[23] **Had you rather ... ?** *Would you rather ... ? – a rhetorical question that can be answered only in the affirmative since it avoids the real question at issue. There is complex antithesis between the two halves of the sentence (living, slaves/dead, free men) and within each half (living/die; dead/live).*

[25-30] **As Caesar ... ambition** *Both sentences elaborate what has already been said by means of an abstract analysis of Caesar's qualities, which contrasts with Antony's intimate description of Caesar as an individual man. Both rise to the same climax and each clause in the second echoes the corresponding clause in the first.*

[30-6] **Who is here ... reply** *The parallelism of these three rhetorical questions is emphasised by the alliteration. Again there can be only one answer.*

[31] **would be** *would wish to be*

[32] **offended** *harmed*

    rude *barbarous*

Those that will hear me speak, let 'em stay
here;
Those that will follow Cassius, go with him;
And public reasons shall be rendered
Of Caesar's death.

FIRST CITIZEN   I will hear Brutus speak.

SECOND CITIZEN I will hear Cassius, and compare
their reasons,
When severally we hear them rendered.   10

[*Exit* CASSIUS, *with some of the* CITIZENS

BRUTUS *goes on to the speaker's rostrum*

THIRD CITIZEN The noble Brutus is ascended;
silence!

BRUTUS Be patient till the last.
Romans, countrymen, and lovers, hear me for my
cause, and be silent, that you may hear. Believe
me for mine honour, and have respect to mine
honour, that you may believe. Censure me in
your wisdom, and awake your senses, that you
may the better judge. If there be any in this
assembly, any dear friend of Caesar's, to him I say
that Brutus' love to Caesar was no less than his. If   20
then that friend demand why Brutus rose against
Caesar, this is my answer – not that I loved Caesar
less, but that I loved Rome more. Had you rather
Caesar were living, and die all slaves, than that
Caesar were dead, to live all free men? As Caesar
loved me, I weep for him; as he was fortunate, I rejoice at it; as he was valiant, I honour him; but, as
he was ambitious, I slew him. There is tears, for
his love; joy, for his fortune; honour, for his
valour; and death, for his ambition. Who is here so   30
base, that would be a bondman? If any, speak;
for him have I offended. Who is here so rude that
would not be a Roman? If any, speak; for him
have I offended. Who is here so vile that will not

[39] than . . . Brutus   *i.e. if he becomes a tyrant. But his unintentional prophecy is ironically fulfilled when the crowd seek his death.*

[39–40] The . . . enrolled   *The circumstances leading to his death are recorded in the archives. There has been no opportunity for this in the play since Shakespeare omitted Brutus's earlier speech in the Senate.*

[41] extenuated   *belittled*

wherein . . . worthy   *which did him honour*

[42] enforced   *emphasised. The antithetical structure continues.*

[46–7] a . . . commonwealth   *his rightful place in a free republic*

[47] as . . . not   *as will all of you*

[48] lover   *dear friend*

[52–7] Bring . . . countrymen   *Brutus has 'satisfied' the crowd, but his republican ideals mean nothing to them – they wish to give their defender from tyranny the same regal honours that had excited his opposition to Caesar.*

[54–5] Caesar's . . . Brutus   *Brutus shall be crowned as he has Caesar's good qualities without the bad*

[61] Do . . . speech   *Do honour to Caesar's corpse and attend respectfully to Antony's speech*

[62] Tending to   *Regarding*

love his country? If any, speak; for him have I
offended. I pause for a reply.

ALL None, Brutus, none.

BRUTUS Then none have I offended. I have done no
more to Caesar than you shall do to Brutus. The
question of his death is enrolled in the Capitol;   40
his glory not extenuated, wherein he was worthy;
nor his offences enforced, for which he suffered
death.

Enter ANTONY *with* CAESAR'S *body*

Here comes his body, mourned by Mark Antony,
who, though he had no hand in his death, shall
receive the benefit of his dying, a place in the
commonwealth, as which of you shall not? With
this I depart, that as I slew my best lover for the
good of Rome, I have the same dagger for myself,
when it shall please my country to need my death.   50

ALL Live Brutus! Live! Live!

FIRST CITIZEN Bring him with triumph home unto
his house.

SECOND CITIZEN Give him a statue with his ancestors.

THIRD CITIZEN Let him be Caesar.

FOURTH CITIZEN   Caesar's better parts
Shall be crowned in Brutus.

FIRST CITIZEN We'll bring him to his house with
shouts and clamours.

BRUTUS My countrymen –

SECOND CITIZEN   Peace! Silence! Brutus speaks.

FIRST CITIZEN Peace, ho!

BRUTUS Good countrymen, let me depart alone,
And, for my sake, stay here with Antony.   60
Do grace to Caesar's corpse, and grace his
speech
Tending to Caesar's glories, which Mark
Antony,

[67] public chair *for orators – see note to III. i. 80*

[69] For . . . sake *On behalf of Brutus – since it is he whom they obey in listening to Antony*
        beholding *indebted*

[70–4] What does . . . rid of him *These comments heard through the general murmur of conversation show the extent of Antony's task in countering the impression made by Brutus.*

[76] gentle *noble*

[77–260] Friends . . . another? '*When Caesar's body was brought to the place where it should be buried he [Antony] made a funeral oration in commendation of Caesar according to the ancient custom of praising noble men at their funerals. When he saw that the people were very glad and desirous also to hear Caesar spoken of, and his praises uttered, he mingled his oration with lamentable words; and by amplifying of matters did greatly move their hearts and affections unto pity and compassion*'. (Plutarch) See p. 6.

[77] Friends . . . countrymen *This is similar to Brutus's opening, but Antony begins with the more intimate term.*

        lend . . . ears *listen to me for a while*

[78] bury *take part in his funeral*

[80] The . . . bones *a proverbial saying, implying covertly that there may have been some good in Caesar that present circumstances will not allow him to reveal*

        interrèd . . . bones *buried (forgotten) when they die*

[83] grievous *heinous*

[84] grievously . . . it *Caesar has paid a severe penalty. The repetition of 'grievous' might excite some sympathy by suggesting that the penalty was at least equal to the crime.*

[86] honourable *Antony seizes on Brutus's self-conscious concern with his honour (see ll. 14–16), although as yet there would be no hint of irony.*

By our permission, is allowed to make.
I do entreat you, not a man depart,
Save I alone, till Antony have spoke.

[Exit

FIRST CITIZEN Stay, ho! and let us hear Mark Antony.
THIRD CITIZEN Let him go up into the public chair.
We'll hear him. Noble Antony, go up.
ANTONY For Brutus' sake, I am beholding to you.

Goes onto the rostrum

FOURTH CITIZEN What does he say of Brutus?
THIRD CITIZEN   He says, for Brutus' sake   70
He finds himself beholding to us all.
FOURTH CITIZEN 'Twere best he speak no harm of
Brutus here!
FIRST CITIZEN This Caesar was a tyrant.
THIRD CITIZEN   Nay, that's certain.
We are blest that Rome is rid of him.
SECOND CITIZEN Peace! let us hear what Antony can
say.
ANTONY You gentle Romans –
CITIZENS   Peace, ho! let us hear him.
ANTONY Friends, Romans, countrymen, lend me
your ears;
I come to bury Caesar, not to praise him.
The evil that men do lives after them,
The good is oft interrèd with their bones;   80
So let it be with Caesar. The noble Brutus
Hath told you Caesar was ambitious;
If it were so, it was a grievous fault,
And grievously hath Caesar answered it.
Here, under leave of Brutus and the rest –
For Brutus is an honourable man,
So are they all, all honourable men –
Come I to speak in Caesar's funeral.
He was my friend, faithful and just to me;
But Brutus says he was ambitious,   90

[92–101] He hath . . . ambition? *Brutus made general judgements with no evidence to support them; Antony avoids making explicit judgements, as yet, but gives specific examples (see ll. 104–5).*

[93] general coffers *public treasury*

[94] Did . . . ambitious? *the first hint of disagreement with Brutus*

[95] When . . . wept *probably untrue*

[97] Yet . . . ambitious *more explicit disagreement*

[98] And . . . man *The repetition must be beginning to make an impression.*

[99] on the Lupercal *on the feast of Lupercal*

[103] sure *certainly. There can be no question of the irony now, which prompts Antony's bland disclaimer in the next two lines.*

[107] withholds . . . mourn *prevents you from mourning. Antony suggests that his only purpose is to persuade them to mourn.*

[108] O . . . beasts *Even beasts would have enough understanding to mourn for Caesar. The tone suddenly becomes more passionate; unlike Brutus, Antony appeals to emotion.*

[109] Bear . . . me *Excuse me. He turns away to weep, working on the crowd's emotions by displaying his own. Whether or not this is genuine or feigned, it gives time for the crowd to reflect on what he has said, and an opportunity for him to observe their response.*

[112–20] Methinks . . . Antony *The citizens respond both to his display of emotion (l. 119) and to his implied reasoning, if in a simple-minded way (ll. 116–17). Throughout Antony's speeches their response by gesture, movement and inarticulate murmurs is as important as their explicit comments.*

[115] I . . . place *a proverbial saying, meaning that all change is for the worse. It is the first suggestion of hostility towards the conspirators.*

[118] dear . . . it *pay dearly for it – a more explicit threat*

And Brutus is an honourable man.
He hath brought many captives home to
    Rome,
Whose ransoms did the general coffers fill:
Did this in Caesar seem ambitious?
When that the poor have cried, Caesar hath
    wept;
Ambition should be made of sterner stuff;
Yet Brutus says he was ambitious,
And Brutus is an honourable man.
You all did see that on the Lupercal
I thrice presented him a kingly crown,   100
Which he did thrice refuse. Was this ambition?
Yet Brutus says he was ambitious,
And sure he is an honourable man.
I speak not to disprove what Brutus spoke,
But here I am to speak what I do know.
You all did love him once, not without cause;
What cause withholds you then to mourn for
    him?
O judgement, thou art fled to brutish beasts,
And men have lost their reason. Bear with
    me;
My heart is in the coffin there with Caesar,   110
And I must pause till it come back to me.

FIRST CITIZEN Methinks there is much reason in his
    sayings.

SECOND CITIZEN If thou consider rightly of the
    matter,
Caesar has had great wrong.

THIRD CITIZEN   Has he, masters?
I fear there will a worse come in his place.

FOURTH CITIZEN Marked ye his words? He would not
    take the crown;
Therefore 'tis certain he was not ambitious.

FIRST CITIZEN If it be found so, some will dear abide
    it.

[119] Poor . . . weeping *probably spoken by a woman – compare I. ii. 272-6.*

[121] mark *pay attention*

[122] But *Only*

[123] stood . . . world *overcome the opposition of the whole world*

[124] none . . . reverence *no man is so humble as to pay him respect. Caesar has been reduced below the lowest of them.*

[125] masters *He adopts their own form of address (see l. 114), so identifying himself with them.*

[126] mutiny *riot. By saying that he will not incite them to mutiny he puts the idea into their minds.*

[128] Who . . . men *now openly ironic*

[130] wrong . . . you *He would wrong Caesar by not refuting the charge of ambition, and himself and the crowd by allowing them to be deceived. By this statement he identifies both himself and Caesar with the crowd, in opposition to the conspirators.*

[133] closet *study*

[134] commons *common people*

[135] Which . . . read *He tantalizes them – the word 'will' is repeated fourteen times between this line and l. 164, in addition to its punning use as a verb.*

[136-41] And they . . . issue *another apparent fulfilment of Calphurnia's dream (see II. ii. 76-90). It is ironic that it should be Decius's interpretation that is substantiated here.*

[137] napkins *handkerchiefs. The preservation of the blood of a saint is again suggested (see note to II. ii. 89).*

[141] issue *children*

[144] gentle *noble*

[145] meet *fitting*

SECOND CITIZEN Poor soul! His eyes are red as fire
  with weeping.
THIRD CITIZEN There's not a nobler man in Rome than
  Antony.   120
FOURTH CITIZEN Now mark him; he begins again
  to speak.
ANTONY But yesterday the word of Caesar might
  Have stood against the world; now lies he
    there,
  And none so poor to do him reverence.
  O masters, if I were disposed to stir
  Your hearts and minds to mutiny and rage,
  I should do Brutus wrong, and Cassius wrong,
  Who, you all know, are honourable men.
  I will not do them wrong; I rather choose
  To wrong the dead, to wrong myself and
    you,   130
  Than I will wrong such honourable men.
  But here's a parchment with the seal of
    Caesar;
  I found it in his closet; 'tis his will.
  Let but the commons hear this testament –
  Which, pardon me, I do not mean to read –
  And they would go and kiss dead Caesar's
    wounds,
  And dip their napkins in his sacred blood,
  Yea, beg a hair of him for memory,
  And dying, mention it within their wills,
  Bequeathing it as a rich legacy   140
  Unto their issue.
FOURTH CITIZEN We'll hear the will. Read it, Mark
  Antony.
ALL The will, the will! We will hear Caesar's will!
ANTONY Have patience, gentle friends; I must not
  read it.
  It is not meet you know how Caesar loved
  you.

[146] You ... men *an ironic echo of Marullus's words (I. i. 37–8).*

[148] inflame *incense*
[149] 'Tis ... heirs *He contrives to indicate the contents of the will in the words he uses to tell them that he will not reveal it – compare his use of the same technique of doing something in the very process of saying he will not do it in ll. 104, 125–7.*

[153] stay *wait*
[154] o'ershot myself *gone further than I should – a term from archery*
[156] Whose ... Caesar *This is a cutting remark, followed by the suavely ironic, 'I do fear it.'*
[157] Honourable men! *Antony's constant repetition has made the phrase abhorrent.*

[162] You ... will? *He manipulates the crowd so that they will force him to do what he wants to do.*

[165] Shall ... leave? *His courtesy contrasts sharply with his later treatment of Caesar's bequests to the common people (see IV. i. 8–9). By descending he identifies himself still more closely with the crowd, and is able to show them Caesar at close quarters.*

[174] far *further*
[176] If you ... them now *Antony intends to use the contents of the will as the climax of his oration, but first he will work up the more disinterested emotions of the crowd. He abandons any pretence of observing the conditions imposed by Brutus.*

You are not wood, you are not stones, but
    men;
And being men, hearing the will of Caesar,
It will inflame you, it will make you mad.
'Tis good you know not that you are his heirs;
For if you should, O, what would come of
    it!   150

FOURTH CITIZEN Read the will! We'll hear it, Antony!
    You shall read us the will, Caesar's will!

ANTONY Will you be patient? Will you stay awhile?
    I have o'ershot myself to tell you of it.
    I fear I wrong the honourable men
    Whose daggers have stabbed Caesar; I do fear
    it.

FOURTH CITIZEN They were traitors. Honourable
men!

ALL The will! The testament!

SECOND CITIZEN They were villains, murderers! The 160
will! Read the will!

ANTONY You will compel me then to read the will?
    Then make a ring about the corpse of Caesar,
    And let me show you him that made the will.
    Shall I descend? And will you give me leave?

ALL Come down.

SECOND CITIZEN Descend.

THIRD CITIZEN You shall have leave.

ANTONY *comes down*

FOURTH CITIZEN A ring; stand round.

FIRST CITIZEN Stand from the hearse; stand from 170
the body.

SECOND CITIZEN Room for Antony, most noble
Antony!

ANTONY Nay, press not so upon me; stand far off.

SEVERAL CITIZENS Stand back! Room! Bear back!

ANTONY If you have tears, prepare to shed them
    now.

[180] That . . . Nervii *Caesar's defeat of the Nervii in Gaul (57 B.C.) was one of his greatest victories, and was celebrated by a particularly magnificent triumph in Rome. The combination of this with the personal recollection, and the intimate detail of the 'summer evening', is very telling, even though the recollection must be invented, as Antony did not accompany Caesar on this campaign.*

[181–7] Look . . . no '. . . *to conclude his oration, he unfolded before the whole assembly the bloody garments of the dead, thrust through in many places with their swords, and called the malefactors cruel and cursed murderers'. (Plutarch) In Plutarch's account, the will was read before Antony began to speak. Of course, Antony could not really have identified each rent – he did not even see the assassination.*

[182] envious *malicious*

[186] be resolved *make sure*

[187] unkindly *cruelly and unnaturally*

[188] angel *favourite – with a suggestion of 'guardian spirit' (see II. i. 66 and note). Caesar's ghost is later described as Brutus's 'evil spirit' (IV. iii. 282).*

[190] most unkindest *See note to III. i. 121.*

[191–6] For when . . . fell *See III. i. 77.*

[192] Ingratitude *The blow of Brutus's ingratitude*

[196] Which . . . blood *Plutarch says only that the base of the statue was drenched with blood, but North, misreading the French version from which he was translating, says that Caesar 'was driven . . . against the base whereupon Pompey's image stood, which ran all of a gore-blood till he was slain. Thus it seemed that the image took just revenge of Pompey's enemy . . .' In the play the implication might be that the statue sympathised with Caesar or that it rejoiced that Pompey's death was avenged – it was believed that the corpse of a murdered man bled in the presence of the murderer. Calphurnia's dream is again recalled.*

[198] Then . . . down *Compare I. ii. 256–7.*

[199] flourished *triumphed, flourishing their blood-stained weapons*

[201] dint *impression*

gracious drops *honourable tears*

[202–3] but . . . wounded *see only Caesar's clothing rent. 'Our' continues the identification of Caesar and himself with the crowd.*

Look . . . here *He flings off the mantle.*

[204] marred *mutilated. It is at this dramatic climax that he first uses the word 'traitors'.*

You all do know this mantle. I remember
The first time ever Caesar put it on;
'Twas on a summer's evening in his tent,
That day he overcame the Nervii.   180
Look, in this place ran Cassius' dagger
    through;
See what a rent the envious Casca made;
Through this the well-belovèd Brutus
    stabbed;
And as he plucked his cursèd steel away,
Mark how the blood of Caesar followed it,
As rushing out of doors, to be resolved
If Brutus so unkindly knocked or no;
For Brutus, as you know, was Caesar's angel.
Judge, O you gods, how dearly Caesar loved him.
This was the most unkindest cut of all;   190
For when the noble Caesar saw him stab,
Ingratitude, more strong than traitors' arms,
Quite vanquished him. Then burst his mighty
    heart;
And in his mantle muffling up his face,
Even at the base of Pompey's statue –
Which all the while ran blood – great Caesar
    fell.
O, what a fall was there, my countrymen!
Then I, and you, and all of us fell down,
Whilst bloody treason flourished over us.
O now you weep, and I perceive you feel   200
The dint of pity. These are gracious drops.
Kind souls, what, weep you when you but
    behold
Our Caesar's vesture wounded? Look you here!
Here is himself, marred, as you see, with
    traitors.
FIRST CITIZEN O piteous spectacle!
SECOND CITIZEN O noble Caesar!
THIRD CITIZEN O woeful day!

[211] About!   *Set about it!*
        Seek!   *i.e. the conspirators*

[217-18] Good . . . mutiny   *Antony resumes his former irony, knowing that this temporary restraint will only increase the violence of the mob.*
[218] Flood of mutiny   *Surge of violence*

[220] private griefs   *personal grievances. While appearing to be offering excuses for them, he implies that the conspirators acted for their personal interests, not for the public good.*
[222] with reasons   *triumphant mockery of Brutus's faith in 'reasons' (see III. i. 221-6, 237; ii. 7, 9).*
[223] steal . . . hearts   *deceive you with appeals to your emotions. With magnificent effrontery he proceeds to disclaim, and to attribute to Brutus, precisely those characteristics of his oratory that have enabled him to triumph over Brutus. In so doing he further identifies himself with the crowd (l. 225) and suggests that he has merely reminded them of familiar facts (l. 231) so that they can draw their own conclusions.*
[226-7] that . . . him   *He unscrupulously exploits his own reputation for irresponsibility and Brutus's trust in his promise (III. i. 245-51), but it is true that Brutus permitted him to speak because he thought him incapable of harming them (see II. i. 185-9).*
[228] wit   *intelligence*
        worth   *authority – the only one of these qualities that Antony may in fact lack*
[229] Action   *Gesture*
        utterance   *delivery*
[230] blood   *emotions*
        right on   *straight out, without rhetorical complications – suggesting that Brutus uses rhetoric to deceive*
[232-3] Show . . . me   *a significant reversal of III. i. 260-1. Antony pretends that he has left them to speak for themselves.*
[235] ruffle   *rouse – as a bird ruffles its feathers in anger*

FOURTH CITIZEN O traitors! Villains!

FIRST CITIZEN O most bloody sight!

SECOND CITIZEN We will be revenged.   210

ALL Revenge! About! Seek! Burn! Fire! Kill!
    Slay! Let not a traitor live!

ANTONY Stay, countrymen.

FIRST CITIZEN Peace there! Hear the noble Antony.

SECOND CITIZEN We'll hear him, we'll follow him,
    we'll die with him.

ANTONY Good friends, sweet friends, let me not stir
              you up
        To such a sudden flood of mutiny.
        They that have done this deed are honor-
              able.
        What private griefs they have, alas, I know
              not,   220
        That made them do it. They are wise and
              honourable,
        And will, no doubt, with reasons answer you.
        I come not, friends, to steal away your hearts;
        I am no orator, as Brutus is,
        But, as you know me all, a plain blunt man,
        That love my friend; and that they know full
              well
        That gave me public leave to speak of him.
        For I have neither wit, nor words, nor worth,
        Action, nor utterance, nor the power of speech
        To stir men's blood; I only speak right on.   230
        I tell you that which you yourselves do
              know,
        Show you sweet Caesar's wounds, poor poor
              dumb mouths,
        And bid them speak for me. But were I
              Brutus,
        And Brutus Antony, there were an Antony
        Would ruffle up your spirits, and put a tongue
        In every wound of Caesar that should move

[237] mutiny *Compare ll. 125–6; he again incites them to violence by saying that he is not doing so. There may be an echo of Luke, xix. 40.*

[244] Wherein *In what way*

[246] You ... will *Nothing shows Antony's mastery over the crowd more clearly: having incited them to 'compel' him to read the will, he so arouses their pity that they forget all about it, and then produces it – as a conjurer produces the card that the audience had forgotten all about – to fortify their mutinous intentions. The solid benefits it offers them will have a more lasting effect than their pity for Caesar.*

[250] several *individual*
      drachmas *silver coins – this was a considerable sum*
[252] royal *generous – recalling his desire for kingship. Compare l. 73.*
[255] walks *garden walks*
[256] orchards *gardens, with fruit-trees*
[257] this ... Tiber *this side of the Tiber*
[258] common pleasures *public pleasure-grounds*
[260] Here ... another *Compare ll. 54–5.*
[261–7] Never ... any thing *'Therewithal the people fell presently into such a rage and mutiny, that there was no more order kept amongst the common people. For some of them cried out, "Kill the murderers," others plucked up forms, tables, and stalls about the market-place ... and having laid them all on a heap together, they set them on fire, and thereupon did put the body of Caesar, and burnt it in the middest of the most holy places. And furthermore, when the fire was thoroughly kindled, some here, some there, took burning firebrands, and ran with them to the murderers' houses that killed him, to set them on fire. Howbeit, the conspirators, foreseeing the danger before, had wisely provided for themselves and fled.' (Plutarch)*
[266] Pluck *Pull*

The stones of Rome to rise and mutiny.

ALL We'll mutiny.

FIRST CITIZEN We'll burn the house of Brutus.

THIRD CITIZEN Away then! Come, seek the conspirators. 240

ANTONY Yet hear me, countrymen; yet hear me
speak.

ALL Peace, ho! Hear Antony, most noble Antony.

ANTONY Why, friends, you go to do you know not
what.

Wherein hath Caesar thus deserved your
loves?

Alas, you know not; I must tell you then.

You have forgot the will I told you of.

ALL Most true. The will! Let's stay and hear the
will.

ANTONY Here is the will, and under Caesar's seal.

To every Roman citizen he gives,

To every several man, seventy-five drachmas. 250

SECOND CITIZEN Most noble Caesar! We'll revenge his
death.

THIRD CITIZEN O royal Caesar!

ANTONY Hear me with patience.

ALL Peace, ho!

ANTONY Moreover, he hath left you all his walks,

His private arbours, and new-planted
orchards,

On this side Tiber; he hath left them you,

And to your heirs for ever-common pleasures,

To walk abroad and recreate yourselves.

Here was a Caesar! When comes such another? 260

FIRST CITIZEN Never, never! Come, away, away!

We'll burn his body in the holy place,

And with the brands fire the traitors' houses.

Take up the body.

SECOND CITIZEN Go fetch fire.

THIRD CITIZEN Pluck down benches.

[267] windows   *window-shutters*

[269] Mischief   *Destruction. The personification recalls Antony's reference to Ate (III. i. 271), as his irresponsible attitude here recalls his savage prophecy.*
      thou . . . afoot   *you have begun*

[271] Octavius . . . Rome   *Octavius did not in fact reach Rome until May –* see p. 7.

[275] upon a wish   *just when I want him*
      Fortune is merry   *Fortune is smiling on us*

[279–80] Belike . . . them   *Probably they have had reports of how I have influenced the people – an ironic understatement*

ACT THREE, scene 3

Antony's mood of cynical amusement is continued by the macabre comedy of this scene. Cinna was a poet of some distinction, and a friend of Caesar's – 'He dreamed that Caesar bad him to supper, and that he refused and would not go; then that Caesar took him by the hand and led him against his will.' (Plutarch)

[1] tonight   *last night*
[2] things . . . fantasy   *my imagination is burdened with things of ill omen*
[3] will   *desire*
[5–12] What . . . best   *This rapid fire of peremptory and irrelevant questions is intended merely to browbeat Cinna.*
   [9] directly   *without hedging*

FOURTH CITIZEN Pluck down forms, windows, any thing.

[*Exeunt* CITIZENS *with the body*

ANTONY Now let it work. Mischief, thou art afoot,
    Take thou what course thou wilt.

Enter a SERVANT

                       How now, fellow? 270
SERVANT Sir, Octavius is already come to Rome.
ANTONY Where is he?
SERVANT He and Lepidus are at Caesar's house.
ANTONY And thither will I straight to visit him.
    He comes upon a wish. Fortune is merry,
    And in this mood will give us anything.
SERVANT I heard him say Brutus and Cassius
    Are rid like madmen through the gates of
    Rome.
ANTONY Belike they had some notice of the people,
    How I had moved them. Bring me to Octavius. 280

                                 [*Exeunt*

Scene 3. *Enter* CINNA *the poet, and after him the*
CITIZENS

CINNA I dreamt tonight that I did feast with Caesar,
    And things unluckily charge my fantasy.
    I have no will to wander forth of doors,
    Yet something leads me forth.
FIRST CITIZEN What is your name?
SECOND CITIZEN Whither are you going?
THIRD CITIZEN Where do you dwell?
FOURTH CITIZEN Are you a married man or a bachelor?
SECOND CITIZEN Answer every man directly.
FIRST CITIZEN Ay, and briefly.   10
FOURTH CITIZEN Ay, and wisely.

JULIUS CAESAR

[12] you were best *it would be better for you if you did*

[13–16] What . . . bachelor *Cinna's reply may express his confusion – he tries nervously to make a joke of the situation at the end – or it might be said with the amused superiority of an intellectual.*

[18] bear . . . bang *get a blow from me. The second citizen is obviously married.*

[20] Directly *This is a pun – he answers directly, and he is going directly to Caesar's funeral.*

[24] For . . . dwelling *Where do you live?*

[26–39] Your name . . . go! *'When he came [to the Forum] one of the mean sort asked what his name was. He was straight called by his name. The first man told it to another, and that unto another, so that it ran straight through them all that he was one of them that murdered Caesar . . . Wherefore . . . they fell upon him with such fury that they presently dispatched him in the market place.' (Plutarch)*

[30–1] Tear . . . verses *The mob is merely out for blood, any excuse will do.*

[34] pluck . . . heart *simply tear his name out of him (even if he is killed in the process) – recalling Brutus's wish to 'come by' the spirit of Caesar – Caesarism, all that the name 'Caesar' means (II. i. 169–70) – even if Caesar is killed in the process. This episode is a macabre burlesque of Brutus's motives in the assassination.*

[34–5] turn him going *send him packing*

[36–9] Tear him . . . go! *See note to III. ii. 261–7.*

Exeunt *Cinna is dragged away and killed off-stage.*

THIRD CITIZEN Ay, and truly, you were best.

CINNA What is my name? Whither am I going? Where do I dwell? Am I a married man or a bachelor? Then to answer every man directly and briefly, wisely and truly – wisely I say, I am a bachelor.

SECOND CITIZEN That's as much as to say they are fools that marry. You'll bear me a bang for that, I fear. Proceed directly.

CINNA Directly, I am going to Caesar's funeral.   20

FIRST CITIZEN As a friend or an enemy?

CINNA As a friend.

SECOND CITIZEN That matter is answered directly.

FOURTH CITIZEN For your dwelling – briefly.

CINNA Briefly, I dwell by the Capitol.

THIRD CITIZEN Your name, sir, truly.

CINNA Truly, my name is Cinna.

FIRST CITIZEN Tear him to pieces! He's a conspirator.

CINNA I am Cinna the poet, I am Cinna the poet.

FOURTH CITIZEN Tear him for his bad verses, tear him   30
for his bad verses.

CINNA I am not Cinna the conspirator.

FOURTH CITIZEN It is no matter, his name's Cinna; pluck but his name out of his heart, and turn him going.

THIRD CITIZEN Tear him, tear him! Come, brands, ho! Fire brands! To Brutus', to Cassius'; burn all! Some to Decius' house, and some to Casca's; some to Ligarius'. Away, go!

[*Exeunt, dragging off* CINNA

ACT FOUR, scene 1

Over a year has passed, but in the theatre the ferocious murder of Cinna by the mob is followed immediately by the planning of political murders by the new rulers of Rome. 'Thereupon all three met together . . . and did divide all the empire of Rome between them, as if it had been their own inheritance. But yet they could hardly agree whom they would put to death: for every one of them would kill their enemies, and save their kinsmen and friends. Yet at length . . . they spurned all reverence of blood and holiness of friendship at their feet.' (Plutarch)

[1] pricked *marked on the list by pricking the paper*

[2] Your brother *Lucius Aemilius Paulus, who opposed the triumvirs, but escaped to join Brutus*

[4] Publius *Shakespeare's addition, although Antony did allow his uncle to be killed*

[6] with . . . him *I condemn him with a mark*

[7] go . . . house *Shakespeare seems to have forgotten that the meeting was in Caesar's house – see III. ii. 273–4.*

[9] cut . . . charge *reduce the expense of – compare III. ii. 248–60.*

[12] slight unmeritable *insignificant and not meriting respect*

[13] Meet *Suitable*
     fit *appropriate*

[14] The . . . divided *when the world is divided into three parts (i.e. between them) – perhaps referring to the division of the Roman provinces between Europe, Africa and Asia*
     stand *remain*

[16] voice *opinion, vote*

[17] black . . . proscription *sentence of death and exile*

[18] seen . . . days *am older, more experienced*

[20] To . . . loads *To relieve ourselves of the burden of reproaches for our actions – i.e. by putting the blame on Lepidus*

[24] will *wish*

ACT FOUR

Scene I. ANTONY, OCTAVIUS *and* LEPIDUS, *seated at a table*

ANTONY These many then shall die; their names are
    pricked.
OCTAVIUS Your brother too must die; consent you,
    Lepidus?
LEPIDUS I do consent –
OCTAVIUS   Prick him down, Antony.
LEPIDUS Upon condition Publius shall not live,
    Who is your sister's son, Mark Antony.
ANTONY He shall not live; look, with a spot I damn
    him.
    But, Lepidus, go you to Caesar's house;
    Fetch the will hither, and we shall determine
    How to cut off some charge in legacies.
LEPIDUS What, shall I find you here?   10
OCTAVIUS Or here, or at the Capitol.

                         [*Exit* LEPIDUS
ANTONY This is a slight unmeritable man,
    Meet to be sent on errands. Is it fit,
    The three-fold world divided, he should stand
    One of the three to share it?
OCTAVIUS   So you thought him,
    And took his voice who should be pricked to
    die
    In our black sentence and proscription.
ANTONY Octavius, I have seen more days than you;
    And though we lay these honours on this
    man,
    To ease ourselves of divers sland'rous loads,   20
    He shall but bear them as the ass bears gold,
    To groan and sweat under the business,
    Either led or driven, as we point the way;
    And having brought our treasure where we will,

[25] turn him off   *turn him loose*

[26] empty   *unloaded, with the suggestion of empty-headed*
shake . . . ears   *a proverbial expression*

[27] commons   *on public grazing land – deprived of his own*
fortune
your will   *as you wish. Octavius answers curtly.*

[28] tried   *tested, proved*

[30] appoint . . . provender   *allow him a supply of food*

[32] wind   *turn, wheel*

[33] His . . . spirit   *His bodily movements controlled by my mind*

[34] in . . . so   *to some degree Lepidus is no more than that*

[36] barren-spirited   *dull, with no initiative of his own*

[36–7] feeds . . . imitations   *devours, seizes on, trivial curiosities,*
artificial devices and second-hand ideas. Many editors alter 'objects,
arts' to 'abject orts', meaning 'rejected scraps'.

[38] out of use   *when they are out of fashion*
staled   *made common, cheapened by familiarity*

[39] Begin his fashion   *He thinks the newest fashion*

[40] property   *tool*

[41] Listen   *Hear*

[42] levying powers   *raising armies*
make head   *raise a force*

[43] our . . . combined   *our allied forces be united*

[44] made   *made sure of. The line may be defective.*
means stretched   *our resources made the most of – compare*
II. i. 158–9.

[45] presently   *immediately*

[46] How . . . disclosed   *To consider how concealed dangers may*
be revealed

[47] open   *obvious*
surest answered   *most securely met and dealt with*

[48–9] for we . . . enemies   *a metaphor from bear-baiting. The*
bear was chained to a stake and attacked by dogs. 'Bayed about' may
suggest 'brought to bay' – compare III. i. 204.

[51] mischiefs   *dangerous thoughts*

Then take we down his load, and turn him off,
Like to the empty ass, to shake his ears,
And graze in commons.

OCTAVIUS   You may do your will;
But he's a tried and valiant soldier.

ANTONY So is my horse, Octavius, and for that
I do appoint him store of provender.   30
It is a creature that I teach to fight,
To wind, to stop, to run directly on,
His corporal motion governed by my spirit.
And, in some taste, is Lepidus but so;
He must be taught, and trained, and bid go
    forth;
A barren-spirited fellow; one that feeds
On objects, arts, and imitations,
Which, out of use and staled by other men,
Begin his fashion. Do not talk of him
But as a property. And now, Octavius,   40
Listen great things. Brutus and Cassius
Are levying powers; we must straight make
    head.
Therefore let our alliance be combined,
Our best friends made, our means stretched;
And let us presently go sit in council,
How covert matters may be best disclosed,
And open perils surest answered.

OCTAVIUS Let us do so; for we are at the stake,
And bayed about with many enemies;
And some that smile have in their hearts, I
    fear,   50
Millions of mischiefs.

                                        [*Exeunt*

ACT FOUR, scene 2

As often happens in this play, the beginning of this scene follows from the last words of the previous one. The drum announces Lucilius's return from Cassius, and summons Brutus from his tent.

[1] Stand ho!   *Halt! Lucillus passes on the order.*

[5] do . . . salutation   *give you courteous greetings*

[6] He . . . well   *He sends his greetings by a worthy messenger*

[7] In . . . officers   *Because his attitude has changed, or his subordinates have acted wrongly*

[8] worthy cause   *sound reasons*

[9] Things . . . undone   *That the things he has done should not have been done. 'Now as it commonly happened in great affairs between two persons, both of them having many friends and so many captains under them, there ran tales and complaints betwixt them.' (Plutarch)*

at hand   *near*

[10] satisfied   *given a satisfactory explanation*

[12] full . . . honour   *fully deserving respect and entirely honourable*

[14] let . . . resolved   *let my uncertainties be resolved*

[16] familiar instances   *evidence of close friendship*

[17] free . . . conference   *open and friendly conversation*

[18] he . . . old   *as he used to show in the past*

[19] hot   *ardent*

Ever note   *Always remember. Brutus again thinks in terms of general maxims – compare II. i. 21–7.*

[21] enforcèd ceremony   *strained courtesy*

[22] simple faith   *sincere, unadulterated friendship*

[23] hollow   *insincere, empty*

hot at hand   *ardent at first*

[24] Make . . . mettle   *Make a fine show and give promise of their spirit and courage*

[25] should endure   *ought to respond to*

[26] fall their crests   *lower their proudly arched necks*

jades   *poor, worn-out, horses*

[27] Sink . . . trial   *Collapse when put to the test*

[28] Sardis   *the capital city of Lydia, in Asia Minor*

Scene 2. *Drum. Enter* LUCILIUS, PINDARUS *and* SOLDIERS;
enter BRUTUS *and* LUCIUS *from Brutus' tent*

BRUTUS Stand ho!
LUCIUS Give the word, ho! and stand.
BRUTUS What now, Lucilius, is Cassius near?
LUCILIUS He is at hand, and Pindarus is come
   To do you salutation from his master.
BRUTUS He greets me well. Your master, Pindarus,
   In his own change, or by ill officers,
   Hath given me some worthy cause to wish
   Things done, undone. But if he be at hand,
   I shall be satisfied.
PINDARUS   I do not doubt   10
   But that my noble master will appear
   Such as he is, full of regard and honour.
BRUTUS He is not doubted. [*Aside to* LUCILIUS] A word,
   Lucilius;
   How he received you, let me be resolved.
LUCILIUS With courtesy, and with respect enough,
   But not with such familiar instances,
   Nor with such free and friendly conference,
   As he hath used of old.
BRUTUS   Thou hast described
   A hot friend cooling. Ever note, Lucilius,
   When love begins to sicken and decay   20
   It useth an enforcèd ceremony.
   There are no tricks in plain and simple faith;
   But hollow men, like horses hot at hand,
   Make gallant show and promise of their mettle;

Low march within

   But when they should endure the bloody spur,
   They fall their crests, and like deceitful jades
   Sink in the trial. Comes his army on?
LUCILIUS They mean this night in Sardis to be
   quartered.

[29] the . . . general   *the main force of cavalry*

[33] Speak . . . along   *Pass on the order. The third soldier might be off-stage to give the impression of a large army.*

[37] Most . . . wrong   *The impetuous Cassius blurts out his complaint.*

[38–9] Judge . . . brother?   *This generalised appeal to his immaculate virtue is equally typical of Brutus.*

[40] this . . . wrongs   *your calm, dignified manner conceals your unjust actions*

[41] be content   *keep calm*

[42] griefs   *grievances*
      do know   *understand*

[46] enlarge . . . griefs   *set out your complaints in full*

[47] give you audience   *listen to you*

[48] charges   *forces under their command*

[50–2] Lucius . . . door   *The Folio has 'Lucilius' in l. 50 and 'Lucius' in l. 52, but at IV. iii. 126 it is Lucilius who is guarding the tent. He is of similar rank to Titinius, whereas Lucius is only a servant, like Pindarus (l. 47).*

The greater part, the horse in general,
Are come with Cassius.

Enter CASSIUS *and* SOLDIERS

BRUTUS   Hark, he is arrived.   30
        March gently on to meet him.
CASSIUS Stand ho!
BRUTUS Stand ho! Speak the word along.
FIRST SOLDIER Stand!
SECOND SOLDIER Stand!
THIRD SOLDIER Stand!
CASSIUS Most noble brother, you have done me wrong.
BRUTUS Judge me, you gods; wrong I mine enemies?
        And if not so, how should I wrong a brother?
CASSIUS Brutus, this sober form of yours hides
            wrongs;   40
        And when you do them –
BRUTUS   Cassius, be content,
        Speak your griefs softly; I do know you well.
        Before the eyes of both our armies here,
        Which should perceive nothing but love from
            us,
        Let us not wrangle. Bid them move away;
        Then in my tent, Cassius, enlarge your griefs,
        And I will give you audience.
CASSIUS   Pindarus,
        Bid our commanders lead their charges off
        A little from this ground.
BRUTUS Lucius, do you the like; and let no man   50
        Come to our tent till we have done our con-
            ference.
        Lucilius and Titinius guard our door.
                                            [*Exeunt*

ACT FOUR, scene 3

*The tent might be either a separate erection, called a 'mansion'
on the Elizabethan stage, or the inner stage under the balcony.
In Plutarch, the dispute lasted two days: '. . . before they fell
in hand with any other matter, they went into a little chamber
together, and bade every man avoid, and did shut the doors to
them. Then they began to pour out their complaints one to the
other, and grew hot and loud, earnestly accusing one another,
and at length fell both a-weeping.'*

[1] doth appear   *is evident*
[2] noted   *punished by public disgrace*
    Lucius Pella   *'Brutus . . . did condemn and note Lucius
Pella for a defamed person . . . for that he was accused and convicted
of robbery and pilfery in his office. This judgement much misliked
Cassius, because he himself had secretly . . . warned two of his
friends, attainted and convicted of like offences, and openly had
cleared them . . '. And therefore he greatly reproved Brutus for that
he would show himself so straight and severe, in such a time as was
meeter to bear a little than to take things at the worst.' (Plutarch)*
[4] praying . . . side   *pleading on his behalf*
[5] slighted off   *contemptuously ignored*
[6] wronged yourself   *put yourself in the wrong*
[8] every . . . comment   *every trivial offence should be criticised*
[10] condemned . . . palm   *accused of being ready to take bribes*
[11] mart   *trade*
    offices   *lucrative positions in your army*
[15-16] The . . . head   *Their association with Cassius gives an
appearance of honour to their corruption, and so they are not punished.*
[18-28] Remember . . . Roman   *'Brutus . . . answered that he
should remember the ides of March, at which time they slew Julius
Caesar, who neither pilled nor polled the country, but only was a
favourer and suborner of all them that did rob and spoil, by his
countenance and authority.' (Plutarch)*
[20-1] What . . . justice?   *Who that touched his body was such a
villain that he stabbed for any other reason than a desire for justice?*
[23] But . . . robbers   *only because he supported robbers. This is
a new charge against Caesar, which Brutus did not mention when considering his murder (II. i. 10-34).*

Scene 3. BRUTUS *and* CASSIUS *enter the tent*

CASSIUS That you have wronged me doth appear in
    this:
    You have condemned and noted Lucius Pella
    For taking bribes here of the Sardians;
    Wherein my letters, praying on his side,
    Because I knew the man, were slighted off.
BRUTUS You wronged yourself to write in such a case.
CASSIUS In such a time as this it is not meet
    That every nice offence should bear his
    comment.
BRUTUS Let me tell you, Cassius, you yourself
    Are much condemned to have an itching palm, 10
    To sell and mart your offices for gold
    To undeservers.
CASSIUS   I an itching palm!
    You know that you are Brutus that speaks this,
    Or, by the gods, this speech were else your last.
BRUTUS The name of Cassius honours this corruption,
    And chastisement doth therefore hide his head.
CASSIUS Chastisement!
BRUTUS Remember March, the ides of March
    remember.
    Did not great Julius bleed for justice' sake?
    What villain touched his body, that did stab, 20
    And not for justice? What, shall one of us,
    That struck the foremost man of all this world
    But for supporting robbers, shall we now
    Contaminate our fingers with base bribes,
    And sell the mighty space of our large honours
    For so much trash as may be graspèd thus?
    I had rather be a dog, and bay the moon,
    Than such a Roman.
CASSIUS   Brutus, bait not me;
    I'll not endure it. You forget yourself,
    To hedge me in. I am a soldier, I, 30

[25] sell . . . honours *sacrifice the high honours that we have gained for the sake of money*

[26] trash *rubbish, worthless money*

[27] bay *howl at* – *a proverbial expression for ineffective action (compare 'shake his ears', IV. i. 26)*

[28] bait *attack* – *as in bear baiting (see IV. i. 48–9)*

[30] hedge me in *restrict my freedom of action*

[31] Older in practice *More experienced in practical affairs. Brutus's errors justify this claim; Cassius has at last lost patience with him.*

[32] make conditions *manage affairs*

[32–64] Go to! . . . for *The quarrel takes on a familiar childish character.*

[32] Go to! *Nonsense!* – *a common expression of contempt*

[35] Urge *Provoke*

[36] Have . . . health *Consider the consequences for your health* – *an implied threat*

tempt *try my patience*

[37] slight *worthless* – *compare IV. i. 12.*

[39] give . . . choler *submit and give free scope to your impetuous temper. Choler was one of the four humours (see note to V. v. 73–4); it was hot and dry.*

[42] Fret *Rage*

[43] choleric *prone to anger*

[44] budge *flinch*

[45] observe you *attend to your every whim, obsequiously*

stand . . . crouch *remain patiently and cringe*

[46] testy humour *irritable temper*

[47–8] digest . . . you *swallow the poison of your own anger even though it makes you burst. The spleen was thought to be the source of anger.*

[48] forth *onwards*

[49] for my mirth *to amuse me*

[50] waspish *vicious. Brutus's sense of superiority is becoming increasingly childish.*

Is . . . this? *Cassius is astounded by Brutus's hardness.*

[52] make. . . true *show the truth of your boasting*

[54] to learn *to take lessons from* – *heavily sarcastic*

[57] If . . . not *a childish pout*

[58] durst . . . me *dared not have so aroused my anger*

> Older in practice, abler than yourself
> To make conditions.

BRUTUS   Go to! You are not, Cassius.

CASSIUS I am.

BRUTUS I say you are not.

CASSIUS Urge me no more, I shall forget myself;
> Have mind upon your health; tempt me no
>   farther.

BRUTUS Away, slight man!

CASSIUS Is't possible?

BRUTUS   Hear me, for I will speak.
> Must I give way and room to your rash choler?
> Shall I be frighted when a madman stares?   40

CASSIUS O ye gods, ye gods! must I endure all this?

BRUTUS All this? Ay, more. Fret till your proud heart
>   break;
> Go show your slaves how choleric you are,
> And make your bondmen tremble. Must I
>   budge?
> Must I observe you? Must I stand and crouch
> Under your testy humour? By the gods,
> You shall digest the venom of your spleen,
> Though it do split you. For from this day forth
> I'll use you for my mirth, yea, for my laughter,
> When you are waspish.

CASSIUS   Is it come to this?   50

BRUTUS You say you are a better soldier:
> Let it appear so; make your vaunting true,
> And it shall please me well. For mine own part,
> I shall be glad to learn of noble men.

CASSIUS You wrong me every way; you wrong me,
>   Brutus.
> I said, an elder soldier, not a better.
> Did I say better?

BRUTUS   If you did, I care not.

CASSIUS When Caesar lived, he durst not thus have
>   moved me.

[63] presume *rely*

[67] armed . . . honesty *so fortified by my sense of honour*

[68] idle *ineffective*

[69] respect not *pay no attention to*

[69–77] I did . . . Cassius? '*Brutus prayed Cassius to let him have some part of his money whereof he had great store . . . Cassius's friends hindered this request and earnestly dissuaded him from it, persuading him that it was no reason that Brutus should have the money which Cassius had gotten together by sparing, and levied with great evil will of the people their subjects . . . This notwithstanding, Cassius gave him the third part of his total sum.*' (*Plutarch*)

[71] vile *despicable. Brutus condemns Cassius for the means he uses to raise money, yet is prepared to claim a share of the money raised by such methods – for the paradoxical reason that he is too virtuous to use such methods himself.*

[72] coin my heart *melt down my heart and cast it into coins*

[73] drop . . . drachmas *turn my drops of blood into coins. Drachmas were Greek silver coins.*

[74] hard hands *suggesting both the hard work by which it had been gained and their unwillingness to part with it*

[75] indirection *crooked means*

[78] Should *Would. Brutus's tone, especially the more intimate use of first names, suggests that his mood is softening.*

[80] rascal counters *wretched bits of metal. A 'rascal deer' was a worthless animal, not worth hunting.*

[84] but *only. Cassius implies that the messenger had misrepresented his reply. He is now making excuses in an attempt to end the quarrel.*

[85] rived *split, broken*

[86] bear *bear with*

   infirmities *weaknesses*

[87] makes . . . are *exaggerates them. Cassius is generously prepared to concede that the fault was his.*

[88] practise . . . me *exercise them against me*

BRUTUS Peace, peace! you durst not so have tempted
    him.
CASSIUS I durst not?   60
BRUTUS No.
CASSIUS What, durst not tempt him?
BRUTUS   For your life you durst not.
CASSIUS Do not presume too much upon my love;
    I may do that I shall be sorry for.
BRUTUS You have done that you should be sorry for.
    There is no terror, Cassius, in your threats;
    For I am armed so strong in honesty
    That they pass by me as the idle wind,
    Which I respect not. I did send to you
    For certain sums of gold, which you denied
      me;   70
    For I can raise no money by vile means.
    By heaven, I had rather coin my heart,
    And drop my blood for drachmas, than to
      wring
    From the hard hands of peasants their vile
      trash
    By any indirection. I did send
    To you for gold to pay my legions,
    Which you denied me. Was that done like
      Cassius?
    Should I have answered Caius Cassius so?
    When Marcus Brutus grows so covetous,
    To lock such rascal counters from his friends, 80
    Be ready gods with all your thunderbolts;
    Dash him to pieces.
CASSIUS   I denied you not.
BRUTUS You did.
CASSIUS I did not. He was but a fool that brought
    My answer back. Brutus hath rived my heart.
    A friend should bear his friend's infirmities;
    But Brutus makes mine greater than they are.
BRUTUS I do not, till you practise them on me.

[89] I . . . faults   *rather grudging; perhaps the brevity of these replies suggests that Brutus is a little shamefaced after Cassius's affectionate appeal for sympathy, and is trying to respond without losing face.*

[92] Olympus   *See note to III. i. 74.*

[94] alone on Cassius   *on Cassius alone*

[96] braved   *defied*
[97] Checked   *Rebuked*

[98] conned by rote   *learned by heart*
[99–100] weep . . . eyes   *die of grief*
[100–5] There is . . . Caesar   *Cassius resorts to a characteristic theatrical gesture to gain sympathy; compare Antony's perhaps more deliberate tactics with Brutus, III. i. 151–63.*

[102] Pluto's mine   *Pluto, god of the underworld, was often confused with Plutus, god of wealth.*

[104] I . . . heart   *i.e. I, that am accused of denying you gold, am ready to give you not only gold but my heart*

[108] it . . . scope   *your anger may have free expression*
[109] dishonour . . . humour   *I will attribute any dishonour you do me merely to a passing mood (see note to II. i. 250). Even now Brutus can only go so far as to say that he will tolerate Cassius's faults.*
[110] yoked   *allied*
[111–13] That . . . again   *i.e. whose anger is only struck from the surface (not deep-seated), like the momentary spark struck from a flint*
[112] much enforced   *struck with force*
[113] straight   *at once*
[115] blood ill-tempered   *indisposition of the blood – due to an excess of choler. See note to V. v. 73–4.*
[117] Do . . . much?   *Cassius is astounded by this first admission by Brutus that he was also at fault.*
[118] O Brutus!   *He is still shaken by the quarrel.*

CASSIUS You love me not.

BRUTUS   I do not like your faults.

CASSIUS A friendly eye could never see such faults.   90

BRUTUS A flatterer's would not, though they do appear
        As huge as high Olympus.

CASSIUS Come, Antony, and young Octavius, come,
        Revenge yourselves alone on Cassius,
        For Cassius is aweary of the world:
        Hated by one he loves; braved by his brother;
        Checked like a bondman; all his faults
            observed,
        Set in a note-book, learned, and conned by
            rote,
        To cast into my teeth. O, I could weep
        My spirit from mine eyes! There is my dagger, 100
        And here my naked breast; within, a heart
        Dearer than Pluto's mine, richer than gold.
        If that thou be'st a Roman, take it forth.
        I, that denied thee gold, will give my heart.
        Strike as thou didst at Caesar; for I know,
        When thou didst hate him worst, thou lovedst
            him better
        Than ever thou lovedst Cassius.

BRUTUS   Sheathe your dagger.
        Be angry when you will, it shall have scope;
        Do what you will, dishonour shall be humour.
        O Cassius, you are yoked with a lamb   110
        That carries anger as the flint bears fire,
        Who, much enforced, shows a hasty spark,
        And straight is cold again.

CASSIUS   Hath Cassius lived
        To be but mirth and laughter to his Brutus,
        When grief and blood ill-tempered vexeth him?

BRUTUS When I spoke that, I was ill-tempered too.

CASSIUS Do you confess so much? Give me your hand.

BRUTUS And my heart too.

CASSIUS   O Brutus!

[120] rash . . . me *choleric disposition I inherited from my mother*

[121] forgetful *forget myself*

[122] over-earnest with *too severe on – a friendly understatement*

[123] leave you so *leave it at that*

[124–38] Let me . . . gone *In Plutarch the Poet interrupts their first day's conference: 'one, Marcus Phaonius, that had been a friend and follower of Cato while he lived, and took upon him to counterfeit a philosopher, not with wisdom and discretion, but with a certain bedlam and frantic motion . . . in despite of the door-keepers, came into the chamber, and with a certain scoffing and mocking gesture, which he counterfeited of purpose, he rehearsed the verses which old Nestor said in Homer:*

My lords, I pray you hearken both to me,
For I have seen mo years than suchie three.

Cassius fell a-laughing at him; but Brutus thrust him out of the chamber, and called him dog, and counterfeit Cynic. Howbeit his coming in brake their strife at that time.'

[125] grudge *ill-feeling*

meet *fitting*

[128] stay *stop*

[133] cynic *Plutarch's description shows that Phaonius mimicked the Cynic philosophers, such as Diogenes, whose contempt for normal worldly values led them into apparently odd behaviour – Diogenes lived in a tub.*

[134] Saucy *Insolent. The Poet offends Brutus's sense of decorum and dignity.*

[135] fashion *manner. Cassius welcomes this light relief after the quarrel.*

[136] I'll . . . time. *I'll make allowances for his whims when he knows the right time for them*

[137] What . . . fools? *What has war to do with – or, what use in war are – these rhyming fools?*

[138] Companion *Fellow – often used contemptuously*

[140] lodge *encamp*

BRUTUS   What's the matter?
CASSIUS Have not you love enough to bear with me,
        When that rash humour which my mother gave
        me   120
        Makes me forgetful?
BRUTUS   Yes, Cassius, and from henceforth,
        When you are over-earnest with your Brutus,
        He'll think your mother chides, and leave you
        so.

Enter POET, *followed by* LUCILIUS, TITINIUS *and*
                    LUCIUS

POET Let me go in to see the generals.
        There is some grudge between 'em; 'tis not
        meet
        They be alone.
LUCILIUS You shall not come to them.
POET Nothing but death shall stay me.
CASSIUS How now? What's the matter?
POET For shame, you generals! What do you mean?   130
        Love, and be friends, as two such men should
        be;
        For I have seen more years, I'm sure, than ye.
CASSIUS Ha, ha! How vilely doth this cynic rhyme!
BRUTUS Get you hence, sirrah. Saucy fellow, hence!
CASSIUS Bear with him, Brutus; 'tis his fashion.
BRUTUS I'll know his humour, when he knows his time.
        What should the wars do with these jigging
        fools?
        Companion, hence!
CASSIUS   Away, away, be gone.
                                          [*Exit* POET
BRUTUS Lucilius and Titinius, bid the commanders
        Prepare to lodge their companies tonight.   140
CASSIUS And come yourselves, and bring Messala with
        you

[144] sick . . . griefs *afflicted by many sorrows*

[145] your philosophy *Stoicism – see p. 14.*

[146] give . . . evils *give way to evils that come by chance*

[147–9] Portia . . . dead *This curt interchange characterises the austere moral attitude of the Stoic. The fact is stated, but in the light of this philosophy it is of no more consequence – although the strength of Brutus's grief, as well as his self-control, is evident.*

[150] 'scaped *escaped*
      crossed *opposed*

[151] insupportable *unbearable*

[152] Upon *From*
      Impatient *Unable to endure*

[153] grief *grieving. Two different constructions are combined here.*

[154–5] with . . . came *news of that came with the news of her death*

[155] fell distract *became distraught*

[156] her . . . fire *'. . . she, determining to kill herself (her parents and friends carefully looking to keep her from it), took hot burning coals and cast them into her mouth, and kept her mouth so close that she choked herself'. (Plutarch) Portia's death shows a similar Stoic fortitude – compare II. i. 291–302.*

      tapers *candles*

[159] bury . . . unkindness *drown all the unnatural malice between us*

[160] pledge *pledge of friendship*

Immediately to us.

[Exeunt LUCILIUS *and* TITINIUS

BRUTUS   Lucius, a bowl of wine.

[Exit LUCIUS

CASSIUS I did not think you could have been so
    angry.

BRUTUS O Cassius, I am sick of many griefs.

CASSIUS Of your philosophy you make no use,
    If you give place to accidental evils.

BRUTUS No man bears sorrow better. Portia is dead.

CASSIUS Ha! Portia?

BRUTUS She is dead.

CASSIUS How 'scaped I killing when I crossed you
    so?   150
    O insupportable and touching loss!
    Upon what sickness?

BRUTUS   Impatient of my absence,
    And grief that young Octavius with Mark
    Antony
    Have made themselves so strong; for with her
    death
    That tidings came. With this she fell distract,
    And, her attendants absent, swallowed fire.

CASSIUS And died so?

BRUTUS   Even so.

CASSIUS   O ye immortal gods!

Enter LUCIUS *with wine and tapers*

BRUTUS Speak no more of her. Give me a bowl of
    wine.
    In this I bury all unkindness, Cassius.

CASSIUS My heart is thirsty for that noble pledge.   160
    Fill, Lucius, till the wine o'erswell the cup.
    I cannot drink too much of Brutus' love.

BRUTUS Come in Titinius.

[Exit LUCIUS

[165] call ... necessities   *inquire into what needs to be done*

[166] Portia ... you   *The characters of Cassius and Brutus are again contrasted. The strength of his emotions prevents Cassius from forgetting Portia – as he was unable to forget their quarrel (ll. 118, 143) – whereas Brutus dismisses the matter stoically and turns to practical affairs.*

[169] power   *force*

[170] Bending ... expedition   *Directing their rapid advance*
      Philippi   *a town in Macedonia*

[171] of ... tenor   *to precisely the same effect*

[173] proscription   *sentence of death or banishment*

[176] Therein   *In that respect*

[181–95] Had you ... so   *It is almost certain that this was Shakespeare's first version of the episode that he subsequently introduced earlier in the scene (ll. 147–57), and that it was included in the Folio text by error. If it was intended that both versions should be included, Brutus would be made to tell a deliberate lie (l. 184) in order to show the fortitude with which he could receive the news of Portia's death, and even if one thinks him capable of this it is unlikely that he would have practised such deception when Cassius knew the truth of the matter.*

[185] aught   *anything*

[188] like a Roman   *with the fortitude expected of a Roman*

[190–2] Why ... now   *Brutus's response is the same as in ll. 147–9, 166, but less convincing. 'Why, farewell Portia' is perhaps too casual and does not convey the same mixture of emotion and self-control; in the earlier passage the emotion was conveyed by what Brutus did not say, but here he goes on to outline the Stoic attitude to death. Compare Caesar's development of the same theme (II. ii. 34–7)*

[191] once   *at some time*

Enter LUCILIUS, TITINIUS, *with* MESSALA

                   Welcome, good Messala.
Now sit we close about this taper here.
And call in question our necessities.

CASSIUS Portia, art thou gone?

BRUTUS   No more, I pray you.
Messala, I have here received letters,
That young Octavius and Mark Antony
Come down upon us with a mighty power,
Bending their expedition toward Philippi.   170

MESSALA Myself have letters of the selfsame tenor.

BRUTUS With what addition?

MESSALA That by proscription and bills of outlawry
Octavius, Antony, and Lepidus
Have put to death an hundred senators.

BRUTUS Therein our letters do not well agree.
Mine speak of seventy senators that died
By their proscriptions, Cicero being one.

CASSIUS Cicero one?

MESSALA   Cicero is dead,
And by that order of proscription.   180
Had you your letters from your wife, my lord?

BRUTUS No, Messala.

MESSALA Nor nothing in your letters writ of her?

BRUTUS Nothing, Messala.

MESSALA   That methinks is strange.

BRUTUS Why ask you? Hear you aught of her in yours?

MESSALA No, my lord.

BRUTUS Now as you are a Roman, tell me true.

MESSALA Then like a Roman bear the truth I tell,
For certain she is dead, and by strange manner.

BRUTUS Why, farewell Portia. We must die, Messala.   190
With meditating that she must die once,
I have the patience to endure it now.

MESSALA Even so great men great losses should
    endure.

[194] I . . . art   *I have as much fortitude in theory*

[195] bear it   *support such grief*

[196] to . . . alive   *as we are still alive, let us get to work. If ll. 181–95 are omitted this would follow the news of Cicero's death, and the touch of matter-of-fact irony would be more appropriate to that than to the news of Portia's death.*

[197] presently   *immediately*

[200] waste . . . means   *exhaust his supplies*

[201] Doing . . . offence   *Harming himself*

[202] full . . . nimbleness   *fully rested, fresh and alert*

[203] of . . . place to   *of necessity give way to*

[205] Do . . . affection   *Retain their friendly attitude to us only because they are compelled to*

[206] grudged . . . contribution   *been reluctant to supply us*

[207] by them   *through their territories*

[208] make . . . up   *increase the number of their troops*

[209] new-added   *reinforced*

[213] Under . . . pardon   *the fifth time Brutus overrules Cassius, again rather condescendingly (compare III. i. 235, II. i. 185) and his third error (see V. i. 1–4). ' Cassius was of opinion not to try this war at one battle, but rather to delay time and to draw it out in length, considering that they were the stronger in money and the weaker in men and armour. But Brutus in contrary manner did . . . desire nothing more than to put all to the hazard of battle, as soon as might be possible, to the end he might either quickly restore his country to her former liberty, or rid him forthwith of this miserable world.' (Plutarch)*

[214] tried . . . friends   *strained our friends' resources to the limit*

[215] brim-full   *fully up to strength*

[217] height   *of our strength, fortunes*

[218–24] There is . . . ventures   *The thought is not dissimilar to that of Cassius (I. ii. 139–41), but while Cassius, the Epicurean, insists on the power of men over their destiny, Brutus, the Stoic, stresses the part played by providence.*

[219] the flood   *high tide*

fortune   *success, prosperity*

[220] Omitted   *Missed, neglected*

[221] bound . . . shallows   *restricted to shallow waters*

[223] take . . . serves   *make use of the movement of the tide when it favours us*

[224] ventures   *enterprises – literally, goods risked in trade*

with your will   *in accordance with your wishes*

CASSIUS I have as much of this in art as you,
  But yet my nature could not bear it so.
BRUTUS Well, to our work alive. What do you think
  Of marching to Philippi presently?
CASSIUS I do not think it good.
BRUTUS   Your reason?
CASSIUS   This it is:
  'Tis better that the enemy seek us;
  So shall he waste his means, weary his soldiers, 200
  Doing himself offence, whilst we, lying still,
  Are full of rest, defence, and nimbleness.
BRUTUS Good reasons must of force give place to
   better.
  The people 'twixt Philippi and this ground
  Do stand but in a forced affection;
  For they have grudged us contribution.
  The enemy, marching along by them,
  By them shall make a fuller number up,
  Come on refreshed, new-added, and
   encouraged;
  From which advantage shall we cut him off 210
  If at Philippi we do face him there,
  These people at our back.
CASSIUS   Hear me, good brother.
BRUTUS Under your pardon. You must note beside
  That we have tried the utmost of our friends,
  Our legions are brim-full, our cause is ripe.
  The enemy increaseth every day;
  We, at the height, are ready to decline.
  There is a tide in the affairs of men,
  Which, taken at the flood, leads on to fortune;
  Omitted, all the voyage of their life   220
  Is bound in shallows and in miseries.
  On such a full sea are we now afloat,
  And we must take the current when it serves,
  Or lose our ventures.
CASSIUS   Then, with your will, go on.

[226] The deep . . . talk   *Night ominously accompanies all the conspirators' decisions, and Brutus's errors.*

[227] nature . . . necessity   *human nature must submit to the need for sleep*

[228] niggard   *satisfy as economically as possible*

[231] gown   *dressing-gown*

[235] Never . . . souls   *May such dissension never separate us again*

[236] Every . . . well   *There is poignant irony in this simple statement, after the news of Portia's death and their enemies' increasing strength. All that is 'well' is their personal relationships, and the scene continues to stress the importance of human sympathy in Brutus's relations with both Cassius and his servants.*

[237] my lord   *Cassius continues to acknowledge Brutus's leadership; Brutus graciously corrects him in his reply.*

[239] instrument   *probably a lute*

[241] knave   *boy, without the more recent pejorative sense*
o'er-watched   *exhausted by staying awake. Brutus is still tenderly considerate to his servants (see also ll. 250, 255–72). The symbolism continues: Lucius is again associated with the relief of sleep (compare II. i. 1–5) which Brutus must deny himself (l. 228), and later with the harmony of music, contrasting with the discord in Brutus's mind.*

We'll along ourselves, and meet them at
    Philippi.
BRUTUS The deep of night is crept upon our talk,
    And nature must obey necessity,
    Which we will niggard with a little rest.
    There is no more to say?
CASSIUS   No more. Good night:
    Early tomorrow will we rise, and hence.   230
BRUTUS Lucius! [*Enter* LUCIUS] My gown.
                               [*Exit* LUCIUS
                Farewell, good Messala:
    Good night, Titinius. Noble, noble Cassius,
    Good night, and good repose.
CASSIUS   O my dear brother!
    This was an ill beginning of the night.
    Never come such division 'tween our souls!
    Let it not, Brutus.

Enter LUCIUS *with gown*

BRUTUS   Every thing is well.
CASSIUS Good night, my lord.
BRUTUS   Good night, good brother.
TITINIUS, MESSALA Good night, Lord Brutus.
BRUTUS   Farewell, every one.
    [*Exeunt* CASSIUS, TITINIUS, LUCILIUS *and* MESSALA
    Give me the gown. Where is thy instrument?
LUCIUS Here in the tent.
BRUTUS   What, thou speak'st drowsily? 240
    Poor knave, I blame thee not; thou art o'er-
      watched.
    Call Claudius and some other of my men;
    I'll have them sleep on cushions in my tent.
LUCIUS Varro and Claudius!

Enter VARRO *and* CLAUDIUS

VARRO Calls my lord?

[247] raise *rouse*

[248] On business *To go on business*

[249] watch . . . pleasure *stay awake to attend to your wishes*

[251] otherwise . . . me *change my mind*

[252-4] Look, Lucius . . . me *This small but revealing detail shows us more of the close relationship between Brutus and Lucius, and the readiness with which Brutus turns from public affairs to scholarship (compare II. i. 7); the leaf is turned down (ll. 273-4) where he was drawn from study by the cares of state. Brutus 'spent all the rest of the night in dispatching of his weightiest causes, and . . . if he had any leisure left him, he would read some book till the third watch of the night, at what time the captains . . . did use to come to him'. (Plutarch)*

[256] hold up *keep open – hold up your eyelids*

[257] touch . . . two *play a few melodies. 'Touch' suggests the softness of the music.*

[258] an't . . . you *if you wish*

[261] urge . . . might *press you to do your duty beyond your strength*

[262] young . . . for *young constitutions require*

[265] If . . . live *increasing the melancholy tone of the scene* a song *a gentle, melancholy one. Lucius gradually falls asleep over his instrument.*

[267] murd'rous slumber *Sleep and death were often associated; here sleep has 'murdered' the song.*

[268] leaden mace *Sheriff's officers carried maces with which they touched persons whom they were arresting, and Morpheus, god of sleep, carried a wand with which he could induce slumber. 'Leaden' suggests the dull heaviness of sleep. The scene has become filled with drowsiness, interrupting the harmony of music ,and with the mysterious atmosphere of night, in preparation for the entry of the ghost.*

[273] leaf . . . down *The historical Brutus, of course, would have been reading from a scroll.*

BRUTUS I pray you, sirs, lie in my tent and sleep;
    It may be I shall raise you by and by
    On business to my brother Cassius.

VARRO So please you, we will stand and watch your
    pleasure.

BRUTUS I will not have it so. Lie down, good sirs;   250
    It may be I shall otherwise bethink me.
    Look, Lucius, here's the book I sought for
    so;
    I put it in the pocket of my gown.

LUCIUS I was sure your lordship did not give it me.

BRUTUS Bear with me, good boy, I am much forgetful.
    Canst thou hold up thy heavy eyes awhile,
    And touch thy instrument a strain or two?

LUCIUS Ay, my lord, an't please you.

BRUTUS   It does, my boy.
    I trouble thee too much, but thou art willing.

LUCIUS It is my duty, sir.   260

BRUTUS I should not urge thy duty past thy might;
    I know young bloods look for a time of rest.

LUCIUS I have slept, my lord, already.

BRUTUS It was well done, and thou shalt sleep again;
    I will not hold thee long. If I do live,
    I will be good to thee.

Music and a song

    This is a sleepy tune. O murd'rous slumber,
    Layest thou thy leaden mace upon my boy,
    That plays thee music? Gentle knave, good
    night;
    I will not do thee so much wrong to wake thee. 270
    If thou dost nod, thou break'st thy instrument;
    I'll take it from thee; and, good boy, good
    night.
    Let me see, let me see; is not the leaf turned
    down
    Where I left reading? Here it is, I think.

Enter . . . Caesar *Brutus does not identify the ghost until V. v. 17, but the audience would recognise it. Plutarch describes how Brutus 'saw a wonderful strange and monstrous shape of a body coming towards him, and said never a word. So Brutus boldly asked what he was, a god or a man, and what cause brought him thither. The spirit answered him, "I am thy evil spirit, Brutus; and thou shalt see me by the city of Philippes." Brutus, being no otherwise afraid, replied again unto it, "Well, then I shall see thee again."'*

[275] taper *candle. It was believed that lamps burned dim or blue at the approach of a ghost. In Plutarch the lamp 'waxed very dim'.*

[277] shapes *gives form to*
monstrous *unnatural*

[278] any thing *any real being*

[280] stare *stand on end*

[281] Speak to *Tell. A ghost could not speak until it was spoken to.*

[282] Thy . . . spirit *the genius of Caesar which is overcoming the genius of Brutus (see II. i. 66 167)*

[288] taken heart *recovered my courage. When challenged a ghost would vanish, as the ghost of Banquo vanishes when Macbeth challenges it (III. iv. 72, 106).*

[289] Ill *Evil*

[292] false *untuned. There is perhaps the implication that the ghost has brought discord into the tent.*

[304] Why did . . . sleep? *There is no indication that either had cried out – Brutus may be trying to discover if he could have been deceived into imagining that some other disturbance was the ghost. 'Brutus called his men unto him, who told him that they heard no noise, nor saw anything at all.' (Plutarch)*

Enter the GHOST *of* CAESAR

How ill this taper burns. Ha! Who comes here?
I think it is the weakness of mine eyes
That shapes this monstrous apparition.
It comes upon me. Art thou any thing?
Art thou some god, some angel, or some devil,
That mak'st my blood cold, and my hair to
    stare?   280
Speak to me what thou art.
GHOST Thy evil spirit, Brutus.
BRUTUS Why còm'st thou?
GHOST To tell thee thou shalt see me at Philippi.
BRUTUS Well; then I shall see thee again?
GHOST Ay, at Philippi.
BRUTUS Why, I will see thee at Philippi then.

                                [Exit GHOST
Now I have taken heart thou vanishest.
Ill spirit, I would hold more talk with thee.
Boy! Lucius! Varro! Claudius! Sirs, awake!   290
Claudius!
LUCIUS The strings, my lord, are false.
BRUTUS He thinks he still is at his instrument.
Lucius, awake.
LUCIUS My lord?
BRUTUS Didst thou dream, Lucius, that thou so criedst
    out?
LUCIUS My lord, I do not know that I did cry.
BRUTUS Yes, that thou didst. Didst thou see any thing?
LUCIUS Nothing, my lord.
BRUTUS Sleep again Lucius. Sirrah Claudius!   300
    [To VARRO] Fellow thou, awake!
VARRO My lord?
CLAUDIUS My lord?
BRUTUS Why did you so cry out, sirs, in your sleep?
VARRO, CLAUDIUS Did we my lord?
BRUTUS   Ay. Saw you any thing?

[307] commend me   *present my regards*
[308] set . . . powers   *order his forces to advance*
      betimes before   *early in the morning, before mine*

VARRO No, my lord, I saw nothing.

CLAUDIUS   Nor I, my lord.

BRUTUS Go and commend me to my brother Cassius.
　　　Bid him set on his powers betimes before,
　　　And we will follow.

VARRO, CLAUDIUS   It shall be done, my lord.

                                        [*Exeunt*

ACT FIVE, scene 1

[1] answered *fulfilled*

[4] battles *armies*

[5] warn *challenge*

[6] Answering . . . them *Responding to our threat before we have pressed it on them*

[7] Tut *Antony tries to dismiss Octavius's self-satisfaction with an expression of contempt.*

I . . . bosoms *I can read their inmost thoughts*

[8–9] could . . . places *would prefer to go elsewhere*

[10] fearful bravery *a display of bravado to conceal their fear*
face *bold appearance*

[11] fasten . . . thoughts *convince us*

[13] in . . . show *with a magnificent display. 'Brutus's army was inferior to Octavius Caesar's in number of men; but for bravery and rich furniture, Brutus's army far excelled Caesar's. For the most part of their armours were silver and gilt, which Brutus had bountifully given them.' (Plutarch)*

[14] bloody . . . battle *red flag, the Roman signal for battle: 'The next morning, by break of day, the signal of battle was set out in Brutus's and Cassius's camp, which was an arming scarlet coat.' (Plutarch)*

[16–20] Octavius . . . so *The right-hand side was the more honourable. Shakespeare briefly indicates the rivalry between Octavius and Antony; Octavius asserts his authority calmly but decisively.*

[16] lead . . . on *lead your army slowly on*

[17] even field *level plain*

[19] cross . . . exigent *oppose me at this decisive moment*

[20] I . . . so *I do not intend to oppose you, but I will do as I said*
Drum *The army enters in martial splendour.*

[21] stand . . . parley *stop and want a preliminary conference*

[22] Stand fast *Halt*
out *leave the ranks*

ACT FIVE

Scene 1. Enter OCTAVIUS, ANTONY *and their Army*

OCTAVIUS Now, Antony, our hopes are answered.
    You said the enemy would not come down,
    But keep the hills and upper regions.
    It proves not so; their battles are at hand;
    They mean to warn us at Philippi here,
    Answering before we do demand of them.
ANTONY Tut, I am in their bosoms, and I know
    Wherefore they do it. They could be content
    To visit other places, and come down
    With fearful bravery, thinking by this face   10
    To fasten in our thoughts that they have
        courage;
    But 'tis not so.

Enter a MESSENGER

MESSENGER   Prepare you, generals.
    The enemy comes on in gallant show;
    Their bloody sign of battle is hung out,
    And something to be done immediately.
ANTONY Octavius, lead your battle softly on
    Upon the left hand of the even field.
OCTAVIUS Upon the right hand I; keep thou the left.
ANTONY Why do you cross me in this exigent?
OCTAVIUS I do not cross you; but I will do so.   20

March

Drum. Enter BRUTUS, CASSIUS *and their Army*;
    LUCILIUS, TITINIUS, MESSALA, *and others*

BRUTUS They stand, and would have parley.
CASSIUS Stand fast, Titinius, we must out and talk.
OCTAVIUS Mark Antony, shall we give sign of battle?

JULIUS CAESAR

[24] answer . . . charge   *counter their attack*

[25] Make forth   *Go forward*

[27–66] Words . . . stomachs   *Such verbal conflicts before battle were common on the Elizabethan stage, and help to compensate for the inadequate representation of the physical conflict.*

[28] Not . . . do   *a jibe at Brutus's love of learning – see II. i. 7; IV. iii. 252–3, 273–4.*

[29] bad   *unskilful – referring to Octavius's inexperience as a soldier*

[30] In your . . . words   *Antony retorts by punning on 'bad', which now means 'evil', while 'good' means 'pleasing', referring to Brutus's flattery of Caesar before he stabbed him.*

[33] The . . . blows   *either, the nature of your blows, or, where you will strike them – referring to his treachery*

[34] Hybla   *a mountain in Sicily, famous for its honey. Cassius refers to the 'sweetness' of Antony's words when he promised friendship to the conspirators, and perhaps to his eloquence at Caesar's funeral.*

[35] Not . . . too?   *There is no question mark in the Folio, but Antony must surely imply that his words can sting – in rousing the crowd against the conspirators – so that they must have robbed the bees of stings as well as honey.*

[38] threat   *threaten – as a bee's buzz gives warning of a sting. Brutus may also imply that his words mean no more than a buzz.*

[39–44] Villains . . . flatterers!   *With the recollection of Caesar's murder, Antony's taunts become more bitter.*

[41] showed . . . teeth   *smiled, flatteringly. An ape bares its teeth in a grin before it attacks.*

fawned . . . hounds   *Caesar also associates flattery with images of fawning dogs and sweetness (III. i. 42–3).*

[43–4] Whilst . . . neck   *Compare III. i. 188.*

[45–7] Flatterers? . . . ruled   *Cassius is similarly stung; this is the only occasion on which he blames Brutus for his errors.*

[46] offended so   *been so offensive to us*

[47] ruled   *prevailed – see II. i. 155–89.*

[48] cause   *business in hand. Octavius, a man of few words, is impatient of this waste of time.*

[49] The . . . drops   *Deciding the argument in battle will turn the drops of sweat into drops of blood*

[52] goes up   *will be returned to its scabbard*

ANTONY No, Caesar, we will answer on their charge.
    Make forth; the generals would have some
    words.

OCTAVIUS Stir not until the signal.

BRUTUS Words before blows; is it so, countrymen?

OCTAVIUS Not that we love words better, as you do.

BRUTUS Good words are better than bad strokes,
    Octavius.

ANTONY In your bad strokes, Brutus, you give good
    words: 30
    Witness the hole you made in Caesar's heart,
    Crying 'Long live! hail, Caesar!'

CASSIUS   Antony,
    The posture of your blows are yet unknown;
    But for your words, they rob the Hybla bees,
    And leave them honeyless.

ANTONY   Not stingless too?

BRUTUS O yes, and soundless too;
    For you have stol'n their buzzing, Antony,
    And very wisely threat before you sting.

ANTONY Villains! you did not so when your vile
    daggers
    Hacked one another in the sides of Caesar.   40
    You showed your teeth like apes, and fawned
    like hounds,
    And bowed like bondmen, kissing Caesar's feet;
    Whilst damned Casca, like a cur, behind
    Struck Caesar on the neck. O you flatterers!

CASSIUS Flatterers? Now Brutus thank yourself;
    This tongue had not offended so today,
    If Cassius might have ruled.

OCTAVIUS Come, come, the cause. If arguing make us
    sweat,
    The proof of it will turn to redder drops.
    Look,   50
    I draw a sword against conspirators;
    When think you that the sword goes up again?

[53] three and thirty   *three and twenty in Plutarch*

[54] another Caesar   *himself, Octavius Caesar*

[55] added . . . to   *increased the slaughter done by*

[56–7] thou . . . thee   *i.e. the only traitors present are on your side*

[57] So I hope   – *that he will not die by traitor's hands*

[58] I . . . sword   *implying that Brutus is a traitor*

[61] peevish   *silly, childish*
    worthless   *unworthy*

[62] masker   *one who wears masks in midnight revelry*

[63] Old . . . still!   *Still the same old Cassius – implying that they are used to ignoring his acid remarks.*

[66] stomachs   *appetitite for fighting*

[67] swim bark   *let the ship sail – i.e. whatever the danger, we must fight*

[68] on the hazard   *at risk*

[71–6] Messala . . . liberties   '*Messala reporteth that . . . [Cassius] took him by the hand and . . . told him in Greek: "Messala, I protest unto thee, and make thee my witness, that I am compelled against my mind and will (as Pompey the Great was) to jeopard the liberty of our country to the hazard of a battle." . . . Having spoken these last words unto him, he bade him farewell, and willed him to come to supper to him the next night following, because it was his birthday.*' (*Plutarch*)

[72] as   *included only for emphasis*

[75] As Pompey was   *at Pharsalia*
    set   *stake*

[77] held . . . strong   *believed firmly in the philosophy of Epicurus – and so would not believe in omens (see p. 19)*

[79] credit . . . presage   *believe in things that are supposed to foretell the future. Compare II. i. 195–7.*

[80–9] Coming from . . . ghost   '*When they raised their camp, there came two eagles that . . . lighted upon two of the foremost ensigns, and always followed the soldiers, which gave them meat and fed them, until they came near to the city of Philippes; and there, one day only before the battle, they both flew away.*' (*Plutarch*) *Amongst other omens Plutarch mentions* '*a marvellous number of fowls of prey, that feed upon dead carcasses . . . which began somewhat to alter Cassius's mind from Epicurus's opinions, and had put the soldiers also in a marvellous fear*'.

[80] former ensign   *foremost standard*

  Never, till Caesar's three and thirty wounds
  Be well avenged; or till another Caesar
  Have added slaughter to the sword of traitors.
BRUTUS Caesar, thou canst not die by traitors' hands,
  Unless thou bring'st them with thee.
OCTAVIUS   So I hope.
  I was not born to die on Brutus's sword.
BRUTUS O, if thou wert the noblest of thy strain,
  Young man, thou couldst not die more honour-
   able.   60
CASSIUS A peevish schoolboy, worthless of such
   honour,
  Joined with a masker and a reveller.
ANTONY Old Cassius still!
OCTAVIUS   Come Antony, away!
  Defiance, traitors, hurl we in your teeth.
  If you dare fight today, come to the field;
  If not, when you have stomachs.
     [*Exeunt* OCTAVIUS, ANTONY, *and their Army*
CASSIUS Why now, blow wind, swell billow, and swim
   bark!
  The storm is up, and all is on the hazard.
BRUTUS Ho, Lucilius, hark, a word with you.
LUCILIUS   My lord.
     [BRUTUS *and* LUCILIUS *talk apart*
CASSIUS Messala.
MESSALA   What says my general?   70
CASSIUS Messala,
  This is my birthday; as this very day
  Was Cassius born. Give me thy hand, Messala.
  Be thou my witness that against my will –
  As Pompey was – am I compelled to set
  Upon one battle all our liberties.
  You know that I held Epicurus strong,
  And his opinion; now I change my mind,
  And partly credit things that do presage.
  Coming from Sardis, on our former ensign 80

JULIUS CAESAR

[81] fell *alighted*

[83] consorted *accompanied*

[85] steads *place*

ravens . . . kites *birds of ill-omen*

[87] As *As if*

sickly *diseased – about to die*

[88] canopy . . . fatal *canopy that presages death – like the canopy over a bier on which the dead were laid*

[90] but . . . partly *only half believe it*

[91] fresh of spirit *cheerful in mind*

[92] constantly *with fortitude*

[93] Even so, Lucilius *Brutus concludes their conversation.*

[93–119] Now . . . well made *This passage follows Plutarch very closely.*

[94] stand friendly *may they be firm in their support*

[95] Lovers *Close friends*

lead . . . age *continue to live to an old age*

[96] rest still *always remain*

[97] reason . . . befall *consider what to do if the worst happens*

[101–8] Even by . . . below 'Brutus answered . . . "I trust (I know not how) a certain rule of philosophy by the which I did greatly blame . . . Cato for killing himself, as being no lawful nor godly act, touching the gods; nor, concerning men, valiant; not to give place and yield to divine providence, and not constantly and patiently to take whatsoever it pleaseth him to send us." ' (Plutarch)

[101] that philosophy *Stoicism – see p. 14.*

[102] Cato *See II. i. 295, and note.*

[105–6] For . . . life *To anticipate the natural end of life in such a way, for fear of what might happen*

[106] arming *fortifying*

[107–8] stay . . . below *await the fate destined by the divine powers that govern us here on earth*

[109] in triumph *See I. i. 33, and note.*

[111–13] Think . . . mind *There is a conflict between Brutus's Stoical principles and his sense of Roman honour. Like Cassius, he changes his views when faced with the prospect of defeat.* 'But being now in the midst of the danger, I am of a contrary mind. For, if it be not the will of God that this battle fall out fortunate for us, I will . . . rid me of this miserable world, and content me with r fortune. For I gave up my life for my country in the ides of March, for the which I shall live to another more glorious world.' (Plutarch)

Two mighty eagles fell, and there they
    perched,
Gorging and feeding from our soldiers' hands,
Who to Philippi here consorted us.
This morning are they fled away and gone,
And in their steads do ravens, crows, and kites
Fly o'er our heads, and downward look on us,
As we were sickly prey; their shadows seem
A canopy most fatal, under which
Our army lies, ready to give up the ghost.

MESSALA Believe not so.

CASSIUS   I but believe it partly,   90
For I am fresh of spirit, and resolved
To meet all perils very constantly.

BRUTUS Even so, Lucilius.

CASSIUS   Now, most noble Brutus,
The gods today stand friendly, that we may,
Lovers in peace, lead on our days to age.
But since the affairs of men rest still uncertain,
Let's reason with the worst that may befall.
If we do lose this battle, then is this
The very last time we shall speak together;
What are you then determinèd to do?   100

BRUTUS Even by the rule of that philosophy
By which I did blame Cato for the death
Which he did give himself, I know not how,
But I do find it cowardly and vile,
For fear of what might fall, so to prevent
The time of life – arming myself with
    patience
To stay the providence of some high powers
That govern us below.

CASSIUS   Then, if we lose this battle,
You are contented to be led in triumph
Thorough the streets of Rome?   110

BRUTUS No, Cassius, no. Think not, thou noble
    Roman,

[113] great a mind   *noble a nature*

[120] For ever . . . Brutus   *The repetition makes the parting a solemn ritual.*

[123–6] Why then . . . away!   *Brutus expresses a stoical resignation to fate, and perhaps his disillusionment with the results of the conspiracy; he wishes only that it should be finished with.*

ACT FIVE, scene 2

Alarum   *a call to arms. As Brutus left the stage at the end of the previous scene, there must be fighting on stage before he re-enters.*

[1] bills   *written orders. Plutarch records that Brutus sent his orders written in 'little bills'.*

[2] side   *the wing of the army led by Cassius*

[3] set on   *attack*

[4] cold demeanour   *lack of ardour*

[5] sudden . . . overthrow   *a sudden assault will overthrow them*

ACT FIVE, scene 3

'*Cassius . . . was marvellous angry to see how Brutus's men ran to give charge upon their enemies and tarried not for the word of the battle nor commandment to give charge; and it grieved him beside that, after he had overcome them, his men fell straight to spoil and were not careful to compass in the rest of the enemies behind. But with tarrying too long also, more than through the valiantness or foresight of the captains his enemies, Cassius found himself compassed in with the right wing of his enemies' army . . . Furthermore, perceiving his footmen to give ground, he did what he could to keep them from flying, and took an ensign from one of the ensign-bearers that fled, and stuck it fast at his feet . . . So Cassius himself was at length compelled to fly, with a few about him, unto a little hill, from whence they might easily see what was done in all the plain.*' (Plutarch)

[1] the villains   *his own men*

[2] Myself . . . enemy   *I have turned against my own men*

[3] ensign   *standard bearer*

That ever Brutus will go bound to Rome;
He bears too great a mind. But this same day
Must end that work the ides of March begun;
And whether we shall meet again I know not.
Therefore our everlasting farewell take.
For ever, and for ever, farewell, Cassius.
If we do meet again, why, we shall smile;
If not, why then this parting was well made.

CASSIUS For ever, and for ever, farewell, Brutus.   120
If we do meet again, we'll smile indeed;
If not, 'tis true this parting was well made.

BRUTUS Why then, lead on. O, that a man might
          know
The end of this day's business ere it come.
But it sufficeth that the day will end,
And then the end is known. Come, ho! away!
                                        [Exeunt

Scene 2. *Alarum. Enter* BRUTUS *and* MESSALA

BRUTUS Ride, ride, Messala, ride, and give these bills
Unto the legions on the other side.

                    Loud alarum

Let them set on at once; for I perceive
But cold demeanour in Octavius' wing,
And sudden push gives them the overthrow.
Ride, ride, Messala, let them all come down.
                                        [Exeunt

Scene 3. *Alarums. Enter* CASSIUS *and* TITINIUS

CASSIUS O, look, Titinius, look, the villains fly.
Myself have to mine own turned enemy:
This ensign here of mine was turning back;

[4] it *the standard*

[5] Brutus . . . early *his fourth error*

[6] on *over*

[7] fell . . . spoil *turned to pillaging*

[11] far *further*

[14–32] Titinius . . . joy '*He saw also a great troop of horse-men, whom Brutus sent to aid him, and thought that they were his enemies . . . ; but yet he sent Titinius . . . to go and know what they were. Brutus's horsemen . . . when they knew he was one of Cassius's chiefest friends, . . . shouted out for joy; and they that were familiarly acquainted with him lighted from their horses, and went and embraced him. The rest compassed him in round about on horseback, with songs of victory.*' (*Plutarch*)

[15] hide *sink*

[19] with a thought *with the speed of thought*

[21] thick '*Cassius himself saw nothing, for his sight was very bad.*' (*Plutarch*)

     Regard *Watch*

[23] This . . . first *See V. i. 72.*

[25] run his compass *come full circle*

     Sirrah *a common form of address to inferiors*

[29] make . . . spur *spur their horses towards him*

[31] light *dismount*

[32] ta'en *taken*

I slew the coward, and did take it from him.
TITINIUS O Cassius, Brutus gave the word too early,
    Who, having some advantage on Octavius,
    Took it too eagerly; his soldiers fell to spoil,
    Whilst we by Antony are all enclosed.

Enter PINDARUS

PINDARUS Fly further off, my lord, fly further off;
    Mark Antony is in your tents my lord.   10
    Fly therefore, noble Cassius, fly far off!
CASSIUS This hill is far enough. Look, look, Titinius!
    Are those my tents where I perceive the fire?
TITINIUS They are, my lord.
CASSIUS   Titinius, if thou lovest me,
    Mount thou my horse, and hide thy spurs in
        him,
    Till he have brought thee up to yonder troops
    And here again, that I may rest assured
    Whether yond troops are friend or enemy.
TITINIUS I will be here again, even with a thought.
                              [Exit
CASSIUS Go, Pindarus, get higher on that hill.   20
    My sight was ever thick. Regard Titinius,
    And tell me what thou notest about the field.
                         [Exit PINDARUS
    This day I breathèd first: time is come round,
    And where I did begin, there shall I end;
    My life is run his compass. Sirrah, what news?
PINDARUS *[Above]* O my lord!
CASSIUS What news?
PINDARUS *[Above]* Titinius is enclosèd round about
    With horsemen, that make to him on the spur;
    Yet he spurs on. Now they are almost on him.   30
    Now, Titinius! Now some light. O, he lights too!
    He's ta'en! *[Shout]* And hark! they shout for
        joy.

[34-50] O coward . . . him 'Cassius, thinking indeed that Titinius was taken of the enemies . . . spake these words: "Desiring too much to live, I have lived to see one of my best friends taken, for my sake, before my face." After that, he . . . took Pindarus with him, one of his bondsmen whom he reserved ever for such a pinch, since the cursed battle of the Parthians . . . ; but then, casting his cloak over his head, and holding out his bare neck unto Pindarus, he gave him his head to be stricken off . . . after that time Pindarus was never seen more.' (Plutarch)

[37] Parthia Asia Minor – see p. 26.

[38] I . . . life I made you swear, as a condition that your life might be saved

[41] be a freeman i.e. by killing his master

[42] search probe

[43] Stand Pause
     hilts hilt

[46] Even . . . thee a recognition of the justice of the revenge. The circular pattern of events, the end returning to the beginning, is again suggested – compare ll. 23–5; V. i. 113–14. In another account Plutarch says, 'He . . . slew himself with the same sword with the which he strake Caesar.'

[48] Durst . . . will If I had dared do as I wished

[50] take note observe

[51-90] It is . . . heart 'Titinius crowned with a garland of triumph . . . came before with great speed unto Cassius. But when he perceived . . . the misfortune that had chanced to his captain Cassius by mistaking, he drew out his sword, cursing himself a thousand times that he tarried so long, and so slew himself presently in the field.' (Plutarch)

[51] but change only an exchange of fortune: 'Brutus had conquered all on his side, and Cassius had lost all on the other side. For nothing undid them but that Brutus went not to help Cassius, thinking he had overcome them as himself had done; and Cassius on the other side tarried not for Brutus, thinking he had been overthrown, as himself was.' (Plutarch)

[54] well comfort greatly encourage

CASSIUS Come down; behold no more.
O, coward that I am, to live so long;
To see my best friend ta'en before my face.

PINDARUS *descends*

Come hither, sirrah.
In Parthia did I take thee prisoner,
And then I swore thee, saving of thy life,
That whatsoever I did bid thee do,
Thou shouldst attempt it. Come now, keep
    thine oath.   40
Now be a freeman; and with this good sword
That ran through Caesar's bowels, search this
    bosom.
Stand not to answer. Here, take thou the hilts,
And when my face is covered, as 'tis now,
Guide thou the sword – Caesar, thou art
    revenged,
Even with the sword that killed thee.
                                          [*Dies*
PINDARUS So, I am free; yet would not so have been,
Durst I have done my will. O Cassius!
Far from this country Pindarus shall run,
Where never Roman shall take note of him.   50
                                          [*Exit*

Enter TITINIUS *and* MESSALA

MESSALA It is but change, Titinius; for Octavius
Is overthrown by noble Brutus' power,
As Cassius's legions are by Antony.
TITINIUS These tidings will well comfort Cassius.
MESSALA Where did you leave him?
TITINIUS   All disconsolate,
With Pindarus his bondman, on this hill.
MESSALA Is not that he that lies upon the ground?
TITINIUS He lies not like the living. O my heart!

[59] was   *spoken with a sad emphasis*

[60] O . . . sun   *The image contributes to the suggestion of events coming full circle, the assassination had been associated with the rising sun (II. i. 106–11).*

[63] The sun . . . set   *Cassius is both a 'son' of Rome and the 'sun' that gave them light; with his death their 'day' is gone.*

[64] dews   *the vapours of night – see note to II. i. 266.*
   dangers   *associated with darkness*

[65] Mistrust . . . success   *Doubt as to the success of my errand*

[66] Mistrust . . . success   *'Good' is stressed – implying that Cassius doubted the very possibility of success; his premonition of failure led him to jump to a hasty conclusion and so caused his death.*

[67] O . . . child   *A melancholy disposition makes one imagine evils that do not exist*

[68] apt   *impressionable – too ready to believe the worst*

[69] soon conceived   *quickly imagined – continuing the personification of Error as the 'child' of Melancholy*

[70] Thou . . . birth   *Happiness never accompanies your birth*

[71] mother   *i.e. Melancholy – which dies when the man suffering from it dies*
   engendered   *gave birth to*

[76] darts envenomed   *poisoned lances*

[78] Hie you   *Hasten*

[82] wreath of victory   *laurel wreath*

[84] misconstrued   *misinterpreted. While Titinius refers only to the immediate situation, his comment could apply to the whole conduct of the conspiracy, recalling Cicero's remark (I. iii. 34–5) on the omens that Cassius interprets so confidently in his own interest (I. iii. 68–78).*

[87] apace   *quickly*

[88] how . . . regarded   *how highly I regarded*

MESSALA Is not that he?

TITINIUS   No, this was he, Messala,
    But Cassius is no more. O setting sun,   60
    As in thy red rays thou dost sink tonight,
    So in his red blood Cassius' day is set.
    The sun of Rome is set. Our day is gone;
    Clouds, dews, and dangers come; our deeds are
      done.
    Mistrust of my success hath done this deed.

MESSALA Mistrust of good success hath done this deed.
    O hateful Error, Melancholy's child,
    Why dost thou show to the apt thoughts of men
    The things that are not? O Error, soon
      conceived,
    Thou never com'st unto a happy birth,   70
    But kill'st the mother that-engendered thee.

TITINIUS What, Pindarus! Where are thou,
    Pindarus?

MESSALA Seek him, Titinius, whilst I go to meet
    The noble Brutus, thrusting this report
    Into his ears – I may say thrusting it;
    For piercing steel and darts envenomed
    Shall be as welcome to the ears of Brutus
    As tidings of this sight.

TITINIUS   Hie you, Messala,
    And I will seek for Pindarus the while.

                    [*Exit* MESSALA
    Why didst thou send me forth, brave Cassius? 80
    Did I not meet thy friends, and did not they
    Put on my brows this wreath of victory,
    And bid me give it thee? Didst thou not hear
      their shouts?
    Alas, thou hast misconstrued every thing.
    But hold thee, take this garland on thy brow;
    Thy Brutus bid me give it thee, and I
    Will do his bidding. Brutus, come apace,
    And see how I regarded Caius Cassius.

[89] By . . . leave *Excuse me. He apologises to the gods for ending his life before the time they have allotted to him.*

a Roman's part *the action expected of a Roman – compare V. i. 111–13*

[90] Come . . . heart *The rhyme emphasises the finality of the action.*

[91–106] Where . . . discomfort us '*Brutus . . . knew nothing of his death till he came very near to his camp. So when he was come thither, after he had lamented the death of Cassius, calling him the last of all the Romans, being unpossible that Rome should ever breed again so noble and valiant a man as he, he caused his body to be buried, and sent it to the city of Thassos, fearing lest his funerals within his camp should cause great disorder.*' (*Plutarch*)

[94–6] O Julius . . . entrails *He echoes Cassius's words (ll. 45–6), with additional reference to Caesar's spirit – compare II. i. 167–70; III. i. 270–5; IV. iii. 275–87.*

[97] where *whether, if he hasn't. He expresses admiring wonder.*

[99] The . . . Romans *the last man worthy to be called a Roman – compare l. 63.*

[101] fellow *equal*

[101–2] Friends . . . pay *i.e. this is a time for action, not mourning*

[103] I . . . time *to mourn – to pay the debt I owe*

[104] Thasos *a Greek island near Philippi*

[105] funerals *funeral ceremonies*

[106] discomfort *dishearten*

[107] field *battlefield*

[108] set . . . on *order our forces to advance*

[110] try fortune *try our luck*

a second fight *According to Plutarch, the second battle was twenty days later.*

By your leave, gods – this is a Roman's part;
Come Cassius' sword, and find Titinius' heart.   90
                                        [*Dies*

Alarum. Enter BRUTUS, MESSALA, YOUNG CATO,
STRATO, VOLUMNIUS, LUCILIUS, LABEO, *and* FLAVIUS

BRUTUS Where, where, Messala, doth his body lie?
MESSALA Lo, yonder, and Titinius mourning it.
BRUTUS Titinius' face is upward.
CATO   He is slain.
BRUTUS O Julius Caesar, thou art mighty yet!
        Thy spirit walks abroad, and turns our swords
        In our own proper entrails.

                    Low alarums

CATO   Brave Titinius!
        Look where he have not crowned dead Cassius.
BRUTUS Are yet two Romans living such as these?
        The last of all the Romans, fare thee well.
        It is impossible that ever Rome   100
        Should breed thy fellow. Friends, I owe more
            tears
        To this dead man than you shall see me pay.
        I shall find time, Cassius, I shall find time.
        Come therefore, and to Thasos send his body.
        His funerals shall not be in our camp,
        Lest it discomfort us. Lucilius come,
        And come young Cato; let us to the field.
        Labeo and Flavius, set our battles on.
        'T is three o'clock; and, Romans, yet ere
            night
        We shall try fortune in a second fight.   110
                                        [*Exeunt*

ACT FIVE, scene 4

*As with the opening of scene 2, the interval between Brutus's
exit at the end of scene 3 and his entrance here might be filled
with fighting, Brutus's troops becoming increasingly exhausted.*

Exit *not in the Folio, but Brutus must leave at the beginning of
the scene (see note to ll. 7–8)*

[2] **What . . . not?** *Who is so basely born that he does not?*

[3–6] **I will . . . ho!** *Plutarch records that the son of M. Cato
refused to fly, 'but manfully fighting . . . , telling aloud his name and
also his father's name, at length he was beaten down amongst many
other dead bodies of his enemies, which he had slain round about him'.*

[4] **Marcus Cato** *See note to II. i. 295*

[7–8] **And I . . . Brutus!** *No speaker is named for these lines in
the Folio; as Lucilius impersonates Brutus (l. 14) it is probable that
they are also spoken by him: '. . . seeing a troop of barbarous men
making no reckoning of all men else they met in their way, but going all
together right against Brutus, he [Lucilius] determined to stay them
with the hazard of his life, and, being left behind, told them that he
was Brutus; and, because they should believe him, he prayed them to
bring him to Antonius.' (Plutarch)*

[12] **Only . . . die.** *I yield only in order to die*

[13] **There . . . straight** *There is ample reason for you to kill me
at once. The reason is given in the next line.*

[16] **Room, ho!** *Make way!*

[20–5] **Safe . . . himself** *Lucilius's speech follows the phrasing of
North's translation of Plutarch very closely: 'Antonius, I dare assure
thee that no enemy hath taken nor shall take Marcus Brutus alive, and
I beseech God keep him from that fortune; for wheresoever he be
found, alive or dead, he will be found like himself.'*

[24] **or . . . or** *either . . . or*

Scene 4. *Alarum. Enter* BRUTUS, MESSALA, YOUNG CATO,
LUCILIUS, *and* FLAVIUS

BRUTUS Yet, countrymen, O yet hold up your heads!
                                                        [Exit

CATO What bastard doth not? Who will go with me?
    I will proclaim my name about the field.
    I am the son of Marcus Cato, ho!
    A foe to tyrants, and my country's friend.
    I am the son of Marcus Cato, ho!

Enter SOLDIERS, *and fight*

LUCILIUS And I am Brutus, Marcus Brutus, I!
    Brutus, my country's friend; know me for
      Brutus!
    O young and noble Cato, art thou down?
    Why, now thou diest as bravely as Titinius,   10
    And mayst be honoured, being Cato's son.
FIRST SOLDIER Yield, or thou diest.
LUCILIUS   Only I yield to die.
    There is so much that thou wilt kill me
      straight;
    Kill Brutus, and be honoured in his death.
FIRST SOLDIER We must not. A noble prisoner!
SECOND SOLDIER Room, ho! Tell Antony, Brutus is
      ta'en.
FIRST SOLDIER I'll tell the news. Here comes the
      general.

Enter ANTONY

    Brutus is ta'en, Brutus is ta'en, my lord.
ANTONY Where is he?
LUCILLIUS Safe, Antony; Brutus is safe enough.   20
    I dare assure thee that no enemy
    Shall ever take alive the noble Brutus.
    The gods defend him from so great a shame!
    When you do find him, or alive or dead,

[25] like himself   *true to himself, to his noble nature*

[26–9] This is ... enemies   *Antony's reply is also taken directly from Plutarch: ' "I assure you, you have taken a better booty than that you followed. For instead of an enemy you have brought me a friend; and for my part, if you had brought me Brutus alive, truly I cannot tell what I should have done to him. For I had rather have such men my friends, as this man here, than mine enemies." Then he embraced Lucilius and ... Lucilius ever after served him faithfully, even to his death.'*

[30] where   *whether*

[32] is chanced   *has turned out*

ACT FIVE, scene 5

[1] remains   *survivors*

10

[2–3] Statilius ... slain   *This is explained by Plutarch: Statilius volunteered to make his way to Brutus's camp through their enemies and showed a torch to signal that all was well, but was killed on his way back.*

[4] the word   *the appropriate word*

[5] in fashion   *is now commonplace. He is contemplating his own suicide.*

[5–29] Hark ... lord   *'Now the night being far spent, Brutus, as he sat, bowed towards Clitus ... and told him somewhat in his ear; the other answered him not, but fell a-weeping. Thereupon he proved Dardanus, and said somewhat also to him; at length he came to Volumnius himself, and speaking to him in Greek, prayed him for the studies' sake which brought them acquainted together, that he would help him to put his hand to his sword, to thrust it in him to kill him. Volumnius denied his request.' (Plutarch)*

[11] ill   *evil*

20

[13] vessel   *person – seen as a drinking-vessel overflowing with his emotion*

[15] list a word   *listen to what I have to say*

He will be found like Brutus, like himself.
ANTONY This is not Brutus, friend; but, I assure you,
    A prize no less in worth; keep this man safe,
    Give him all kindness. I had rather have
    Such men my friends than enemies. Go on,
    And see where Brutus be alive or dead;   30
    And bring us word unto Octavius' tent
    How every thing is chanced.

                              [Exeunt

Scene 5. *Enter* BRUTUS, DARDANIUS, CLITUS, STRATO, *and*
                    VOLUMNIUS

BRUTUS Come poor remains of friends, rest on this
    rock.
CLITUS Statilius showed the torch-light, but, my lord,
    He came not back; he is or ta'en or slain.
BRUTUS Sit thee down, Clitus. Slaying is the word;
    It is a deed in fashion. Hark thee, Clitus.

                        Whispers

CLITUS What, I, my lord? No, not for all the world.
BRUTUS Peace then, no words.
CLITUS   I'll rather kill myself.
BRUTUS Hark thee, Dardanius.

                        Whispers

DARDANIUS   Shall I do such a deed?
CLITUS O Dardanius!
DARDANIUS O Clitus!   10
CLITUS What ill request did Brutus make to thee?
DARDANIUS To kill him, Clitus. Look, he meditates.
CLITUS Now is that noble vessel full of grief,
    That it runs over even at his eyes.
BRUTUS Come hither, good Volumnius; list a word.
VOLUMNIUS What says my lord?

[17–19] The ghost . . . fields *'The second battle being at hand, this spirit appeared again unto him, but spake never a word. Thereupon Brutus, knowing he should die, did put himself to all hazard in battle.'* (Plutarch)

[20] hour *hour of death*

[22] the world . . . goes *how things turn out in this world*

[23] pit *the pit to which animals are driven to be trapped, with an allusion to the grave*

[24] worthy *honourable*

[25] tarry *linger*

[27] Even . . . prithee *Just for the sake of that old friendship of ours, I beg you*

[29] office *task*
Alarum still *The noise of battle grows louder.*

[30–8] Fly . . . unto *'. . . one of them said, there was no tarrying for them there, but that they must needs fly. Then Brutus, rising up, "We must fly indeed," said he, "but it must be with our hands, not with our feet." Then taking every man by the hand, he said these words unto them with a cheerful countenance: "It rejoiceth my heart, that not one of my friends hath failed me at my need, and I do not complain of my fortune, but only for my country's sake; for, as for me, I think myself happier than they that have overcome, considering that I leave a perpetual fame of virtue and honesty, the which our enemies the conquerors shall never attain unto by force or money . . .".'* (Plutarch)

[32] Strato . . . asleep *Strato does not know that Brutus's other attendants have refused to help him commit suicide.*

[34] joy *rejoice*

[36–7] glory . . . More *more glory by this defeat*

[38] vile *evil*

[41] Night . . . eyes *darkness (both of the night and of death) weighs down my eyelids*

[42] but . . . hour *laboured only to reach the hour of death. For the Stoic, the peace of death was the reward for an honourable life.*

BRUTUS   Why this, Volumnius:
>The ghost of Caesar hath appeared to me
>Two several times by night; at Sardis once,
>And this last night, here in Philippi fields.
>I know my hour is come.

VOLUMNIUS   Not so, my lord.   20
BRUTUS Nay, I am sure it is, Volumnius.
>Thou seest the world, Volumnius, how it goes;
>Our enemies have beat us to the pit.

Low alarums

>It is more worthy to leap in ourselves,
>Than tarry till they push us. Good Volumnius,
>Thou know'st that we two went to school
>   together;
>Even for that our love of old, I prithee
>Hold thou my sword-hilts, whilst I run on it.
VOLUMNIUS That's not an office for a friend, my lord.

Alarum still

CLITUS Fly, fly, my lord, there is no tarrying here.   30
BRUTUS Farewell to you; and you; and you,
>   Volumnius.
>Strato, thou hast been all this while asleep;
>Farewell to thee too, Strato. Countrymen,
>My heart doth joy that yet in all my life
>I found no man but he was true to me.
>I shall have glory by this losing day,
>More than Octavius and Mark Antony
>By this vile conquest shall attain unto.
>So fare you well at once; for Brutus' tongue
>Hath almost ended his life's history.   40
>Night hangs upon mine eyes; my bones would
>   rest,
>That have but laboured to attain this hour.

Alarum. Cry within, 'Fly, fly, fly!'

[44–8] I prithee . . . Strato? '. . . he went a little aside with two or three only, among the which Strato was one . . . and taking his sword by the hilt with both his hands, and falling down upon the point of it, ran himself through. Others say that not he, but Strato . . . held the sword in his hand and turned his head aside, and that Brutus fell down upon it, and so ran himself through.' (Plutarch)

[45] respect   reputation

[46] smatch   touch

[50] Caesar . . . still   Like Cassius, (V. iii. 45–6) Brutus sees his death as Caesar's revenge; his spirit can now rest.

[51] so . . . will   so willingly

Retreat   trumpet call to signal the end of battle

[55] but . . . him   only burn his corpse on a funeral pyre

[56] only . . . himself   was overcome, killed, only by himself

[59] Lucilius' saying   See V. iv. 21–2.

[60] entertain   receive them into my service

[61] bestow   spend

[62] prefer   recommend

[67] latest . . . master   last service for Brutus. 'Messala, that had been Brutus's great friend, became afterwards Octavius Caesar's friend; so . . . he brought Strato . . . unto him, and weeping said: "Caesar, behold, here is he that did the last service to my Brutus."' (Plutarch)

[68–75] This was . . . man   'Antony spake it openly divers times, that he thought that of all of them that had slain Caesar, there was none but Brutus only that was moved to do it as thinking the act commendable of itself; but that all the other conspirators did conspire his death for some private malice or envy.' (Plutarch)

CLITUS Fly, my lord, fly.

BRUTUS   Hence! I will follow.

    [*Exeunt* CLITUS, DARDANIUS, *and* VOLUMNIUS

    I prithee, Strato, stay thou by thy lord.

    Thou art a fellow of a good respect;

    Thy life hath had some smatch of honour in it.

    Hold then my sword, and turn away thy face,

    While I do run upon it. Wilt thou, Strato?

STRATO Give me your hand first. Fare you well, my lord.

BRUTUS Farewell, good Strato. [*Runs on his sword*]

    Caesar, now be still;   50

    I killed not thee with half so good a will.

                             [*Dies*

Alarum. Retreat. Enter OCTAVIUS, ANTONY, MESSALA,
              LUCILIUS *and the Army*

OCTAVIUS What man is that?

MESSALA My master's man. Strato, where is thy master?

STRATO Free from the bondage you are in, Messala.

    The conquerors can but make a fire of him;

    For Brutus only overcame himself,

    And no man else hath honour by his death.

LUCILIUS So Brutus should be found. I thank thee, Brutus,

    That thou hast proved Lucilius' saying true.

OCTAVIUS All that served Brutus, I will entertain them.   60

    Fellow, wilt thou bestow thy time with me?

STRATO Ay, if Messala will prefer me to you.

OCTAVIUS Do so, good Messala.

MESSALA How died my master, Strato?

STRATO I held the sword, and he did run on it.

MESSALA Octavius, then take him to follow thee,

    That did the latest service to my master.

ANTONY This was the noblest Roman of them all.

[69] save *except*

[71–2] in . . . them *became one of the conspirators from an
honest belief that he was contributing to the general welfare and
common good of all Romans*

[73] gentle *noble*

[73–4] the elements . . . him *his qualities were so well balanced.
The 'elements' were fire, air, water and earth; according to medieval
physiology they were transformed in the body into the corresponding
'humours' – choler, blood, melancholy, phlegm – which were thought
to determine a man's temperament and physical appearance ('complexion') as they were differently 'tempered' or mixed ('complexed').
In an ideal character they were combined in equal proportions.*

[74–5] stand . . . man *proudly declare that this was an ideal of
manhood*

[76] According . . . him *Let us treat him with the honour he
deserves*

[79] Most . . . soldier *With full military honours*

[80] field *army*

[81] part *share*

All the conspirators save only he
Did that they did in envy of great Caesar;   70
He only, in a general honest thought
And common good to all, made one of them.
His life was gentle, and the elements
So mixed in him that Nature might stand up
And say to all the world, 'This was a man.'
OCTAVIUS According to his virtue let us use him,
With all respect, and rites of burial.
Within my tent his bones tonight shall lie,
Most like a soldier, ordered honourably.
So call the field to rest, and let's away,   80
To part the glories of this happy day.

[*Exeunt*

Shakespeare Interviews

devised, written and directed by Robert Tanitch

Four tapes, each of which contains a brief introduction to
one of Shakespeare's most popular plays, followed by a
searching interview with the main characters in the play.
The actions and motives of the characters, and the conflict
and drama of their relationships are revealed through the
interviewer's skilful questioning.

Shakespeare Interviews can be enjoyed both at a simple
and a sophisticated level. For the student coming to
Shakespeare for the first time, these tapes will be invaluable
in helping him to overcome the initial language barrier.
For the student of Shakespeare at CSE, O and A level who
is familiar with the play which he is studying, these tapes
offer a stimulating approach, and a springboard for new
ideas.

Characters interviewed:
Macbeth: Macbeth, Lady Macbeth
Julius Caesar: Brutus, Cassius, Julius Caesar, Mark Antony
Hamlet: Hamlet, Ophelia, Polonius, Claudius, Gertrude
Romeo and Juliet: Romeo, Juliet, Mercutio, Friar Lawrence,
the Nurse

Macbeth	open reel 0 333 15111 9	cassette 0 333 15373 1
Julius Caesar	open reel 0 333 15112 7	cassette 0 333 15375 8
Hamlet	open reel 0 333 15113 5	cassette 0 333 15376 6
Romeo and Juliet	open reel 0 333 15114 3	cassette 0 333 15377 4